WENSLEY CLARKSON is one of Britain's most knowledgeable writers when it comes to the criminal underworld. His books have been published in more than thirty countries and sold more than one and a half million copies. He has also written movie screenplays and made numerous TV documentaries in the UK, US and Spain.

www.wensleyclarkson.com

D1399499

HASH

The Secret and Chilling Story Behind the Drug's Deadly Underworld

WENSLEY CLARKSON

Quercus

First published in Great Britain in 2013 by
Quercus Editions Ltd

This paperback edition published in 2014 by
Quercus Editions Ltd
55 Baker Street
Seventh Floor, South Block
London
W1U 8EW

A CIP catalogue record for this book is available
from the British Library

PB ISBN 978 1 78206 199 1
EBOOK ISBN 978 1 78206 198 4

10 9 8 7 6 5 4

Text designed and typeset by Ellipsis Digital Ltd, Glasgow

Printed and bound in Great Britain by Clays Ltd, Elcograf S.p.A.

What are kingdoms but gangs of criminals on a large scale? What are criminal gangs but petty kingdoms? A gang is a group of men under the command of a leader, bound by a compact of association, in which the plunder is divided according to an agreed convention. If this villainy wins so many recruits from the ranks of the demoralised that it acquires territory, establishes a base, captures cities and subdues people, it openly arrogates itself the title of kingdom.

– Saint Augustine

To Zaid, who paid the ultimate price for dealing in hash.

CONTENTS

PART FOUR
HASH IN THE UK

PART FIVE
LAW ENFORCEMENT

PART SIX
HASH – ON A GLOBAL SCALE

4.4 per cent of the world's population consumes marijuana – about 190 million people – and 0.6 per cent use it on a daily basis (22.5 million people).

Marijuana is a highly lucrative cash crop with a worldwide value of $35.8 billion. That exceeds the combined value of corn ($23.3 billion) and wheat ($7.5 billion).

Cannabis has the greatest non-medical usage of all the drugs in the UK controlled under the Misuse of Drugs Act. Overall, about 10 million people in the UK admit having tried it, with at least 1.25 million regular users. Over a third of 16–24 year olds, or around 2.3 million people, have taken it at least once in their lifetimes.

INTRODUCTION

Welcome to HASH, renowned as the world's most socially acceptable recreational drug. Yet its illicit tentacles spread across the globe, financing everyone from poverty-stricken farmers to professional criminals. Hash is a business worth many billions of dollars a year with a truly dark and sinister side; fuelled by a chilling underworld network of dealers, gangsters, drug barons, crooked cops and even terrorists using sex, intimidation, bribery and murder in their quest for vast profits.

It's reckoned that hash provides the biggest single source of actual income for organised crime across the globe.

The world's law enforcers are failing to eradicate it from our streets because they tend to target other more lethal, so-called harder drugs. As a result, the hash business goes from strength to strength.

Even the United Nations admits that its attempts at hash eradication programmes have dismally failed. Authorities often resort to law enforcement crackdowns without implementing any economic or development measures to help cannabis farmers cope with the sudden loss of income. Officials are supposed to conduct alternative development projects in the areas targeted by the eradication measures. But, more often than not, no economic help is received by the farmers, meaning they often go back to producing hash in order to survive.

So what is hash and how has it hooked so many hundreds of millions of people around the world?

Hash is essentially a concentrated form of cannabis, made from the resin of the female cannabis plant. It is consumed for the effects of delta-9-tetrahydrocannabinol, THC, which causes a euphoric high in the user. Hash can contain up to 35 per cent THC, while other forms of marijuana usually only have between 5 and 15 per cent. The strength of hash depends on the strength of the marijuana from which it is produced.

Smokers of hash say it alters sensory experiences and perceptions of reality and insist it is harmless. Critics say regular consumption can cause psychological dependency and destroy people's motivational senses.

Hash can be produced through two different processes, depending on techniques employed in various parts of the world. In Morocco, the resin glands of the cannabis inflorescence – where its main psychoactive substance, tetrahydrocannabinol THC is concentrated – are collected by sieving when the plant has been harvested and dried. Sieving is also favoured in the Bekaa Valley, in Lebanon, where Lebanese Red hashish was renowned for its high quality up until the early 1990s, when the violence in the Middle East slowed down production.

The other technique for producing hash – used in some parts of Asia – is hand rubbing. Much less technical than sieving, it consists of rubbing the flowering cannabis branches back and forth between the palms and fingers until the resin builds up on the hands. This process occurs mainly in India, including Kashmir, and Nepal.

But sieved hash is much easier and faster to obtain than hand-rubbed hash. One kilogram of sieved hashish can be collected in only a few hours versus 10 to 25 grams of hand-rubbed hashish by one collector during a full working day. Sieving also makes hash more potent because almost no resin is left on the plant.

My interest in unravelling hash's secret criminal underworld began more than twenty years ago when I was investigating the activities of one of Britain's most notorious professional criminals. This man had been a London bank robber back in the 1980s but one of his oldest associates explained to me that cannabis was where this character – we'll call him 'H' – had made his biggest fortune. 'Going across the pavement' – as robbery was known in London in the 1970s and '80s – was a far more risky crime. Drugs were where the really big money could be made and 'H' insisted on dealing only in cannabis because he believed the authorities would be more lenient with him if he was caught. UK authorities had already started coming down hard on cocaine and heroin, so 'H' believed cannabis was much 'safer' for him. And, as I was to eventually discover, the profits he could make from hash were one hundred times that of any robbery.

So, I gradually began to unpeel a layer of the underworld that has existed very much beneath the radar for the past forty years. Those inquiries would eventually take me to many parts of the world because the influence of hash is truly global.

Many people I know simply shrug their shoulders at the mere mention of hash as if it is barely worth anyone's attention, which perfectly sums up the way this illicit industry has been allowed to balloon into a multi-billion-dollar worldwide drugs network. The authorities are often too stretched to prioritise capturing hash gangs and, as a result, its availability has continued unchecked. As one old-time British criminal told me: 'Most police forces aren't that interested in hash and the villains like to make out it is virtually harmless.'

Yet most of the world's hash is produced in some of its poorest nations where farmers can survive only if they cultivate cannabis. Many of these farmers say they would much prefer to be growing vegetables or herd cattle but hash provides them with a guaranteed income, which nothing else can do.

In Morocco's Rif Mountains, for example, lives a population the size of Wales and it is estimated that at least 70 per cent of those inhabitants rely on hash for their income. Many believe the Moroccan government has deliberately 'stepped back' and allowed the area to virtually govern itself because the hash business employs such a big chunk of the population.

It is also clear that cannabis crops in many of the world's so-called troublespots help finance terrorism. In Afghanistan, for example, the Taliban have a stranglehold over hash production because it helps feed and arm that war-torn country's deadly insurgents. Hash is relatively easy to grow and the farmers know that even extreme bouts of weather are unlikely to ruin their crop.

Experts believe that pressure put on the cannabis farmers by gangsters and terrorists has led to the worldwide output of cannabis almost doubling in the past 20 years.

One of the first cannabis smugglers I ever met was a professional criminal called Tony from Kent, in south-east England. He'd set up a 'removal firm' with another gangster's backing and began shipping cannabis in from Afghanistan and Turkey almost forty years ago. It was a perilous drive back then and still is to this day. Tony's employees continue to drive the 10,000-mile round trip because the profits from hash remain sky high.

Tony and his secretive group of hardened professional backers are virtually guaranteed that their 'cash investment' will give them a return of five times the original amount within a month of the shipment arriving back in the UK. 'It's just a commodity to me and I run a business, which needs to make profit. It's as simple as that,' says Tony.

Across the world there are many other examples of massive

hash shipments financed by the underworld. Tony's trucks always carry legitimate goods such as fruit and vegetables as cover, which are themselves often sold in the UK for an extra, healthy profit.

Yet as I've probed further and further into the hash business, I've come to realise the risks are just as deadly as for any of the Class A drugs. I've been told of hitmen paid to kill rival criminals who dared to encroach into another gang's cannabis territory. I've found myself feeling just as uneasy in the company of hash barons as any Colombian cocaine dealers or Turkish heroin smugglers.

I came across a Dutch yachtsman called Jak, who said he had a price on his head because the boat he used to smuggle hash had sunk in an accident off the coast of Majorca, with the loss of the lives of his two best mates. He explained: 'That hash shipment was my responsibility and the criminals who paid for it are still after me because they believe that I owe them the cost of the entire shipment, even though it's lying at the bottom of the sea alongside the bodies of my two friends.'

It's five years since that tragic accident, but Jak believes he still has that underworld price on his head and he continues to watch his back and move house once every few months. 'I've got no choice. If I went to see them to ask them to let me off, they'd probably shoot me dead on the spot. As far as they're concerned that shipment was my responsibility and unless I pay them back the full value of the hash, then they will continue to try and hunt me down.'

INTRODUCTION

So, the violence committed in the name of the hash trade is as cold-blooded and senseless as every other heavyweight criminal enterprise, it seems. Another hash smuggler called Billy, an expat Brit living in southern Spain, told me how he was cornered in an English bar near Marbella and beaten by two men with baseball bats after he was suspected of talking too loudly about his hash baron bosses.

Billy shrugged his shoulders as he explained how he was attacked in the middle of the bar in full view of all the customers. Eventually they dragged him outside into the street where they 'beat me to a pulp' and then left him semi-conscious in the gutter for all to see. It was a classic criminal reprisal, deliberately done in public so that anyone who might be stupid enough to talk openly about the gang would get the message loud and clear that they should keep their mouths shut.

Numerous other examples of the violent, destructive side of the hash business have emerged while researching this book. The cast of characters expanded as it became increasingly clear that hash's criminal influence spread across the world and affects a vast range of people from all classes and backgrounds. Ultimately, most of it is down to one driving force; the major league criminals are only interested in securing the maximum profits, irrelevant of the hardship and danger for those producing and smuggling the actual drug. They see hash as a business like any other. And if they can't guarantee themselves a fat profit, then they'll happily mix the hash with anything to 'stretch it out' in order to retain those big profits.

There is a common misconception among recreational drug users that cannabis resin is always 100 per cent pure. It's complete nonsense, as any hash baron will tell you, *off the record*. Cocaine users have come to expect their produce to be laced with all sorts of things from baby laxative to flour. Ask a hash smoker the same question, however, and he or she will almost always say they like hash in part because they know it's pure. Yet by the time hash usually reaches many smokers in the West, it has often been 'watered down' by up to 50 per cent. Everything from bits of plastic to strips of tree bark have been known to be used to stretch out the profits for the hash gangsters.

It's ironic when you consider that most hash farmers see themselves as hardworking people who pride themselves on the quality of their crop and who shrug their shoulders with a sense of apathy when they hear about the vast profits being made off the back of their 'product'.

So perhaps not so surprisingly, behind most farmers there is a middle man, who usually has close criminal connections in nearby cities. He negotiates the prices paid to the farmers and then uses teams of smugglers, who will handle the drug's journey across oceans and borders.

Often those same middlemen own the land that the farmers grow the cannabis on, which gives them even more control over the product. They in turn are often financed by local drug lords. In many of the world's biggest hash producing countries there are even local politicians – and sometimes governmental officials – involved in 'waving through' the hash when it makes its way from the countryside into the cities and ports.

And relationships between the gangsters and their smugglers can frequently be tense. The smugglers are often led by foreigners, who come from the country where the hash is eventually going to be delivered.

One Scotsman I met called Geoff spent five years working as a smuggler in Morocco's notorious Rif Mountains – the world's biggest producer of hash. He described being a smuggler as 'the worst fucking job in the world'. Geoff explained: 'I had the Moroccans trying to con me every inch of the way and I had a paranoid cokehead of a gangster back in London accusing me of ripping him off. I hated it.'

Inside the twisted criminal underworld of hash it's always best not to presume anything. Most of these characters live by their wits and know that their next shipment could well be their last. A lot of the criminals I came across had records for violence and robbery and involvement in heavier drugs, such as cocaine and heroin.

At the very top of the criminal ladder, there are a small number of kingpins making tens of millions of dollars each year out of hash. Most of these faceless gangsters lead through fear and intimidation, especially of their own workforce. They also often pride themselves on not even touching the drugs themselves, which makes them 'clever' in underworld terms.

Yet a surprisingly large number of criminals at the lower end of the underworld ladder smoke hash themselves. Many are so heavily into it that it is undoubtedly affecting their ability to operate in a criminal environment. The money that many of these villains boast they have made from hash often doesn't stack up when you find them living in seedy rented accommodation in rundown city slums.

As someone who's never particularly enjoyed smoking cannabis it's been awkward to refuse the offer of a joint and sometimes, in the name of 'research', I have succumbed because it would be considered offensive if I didn't sample the 'product'.

Take Irishman Sean. He was the son of one of Ireland's richest criminals and was very upset when I refused a toke of his joint after saying I was about to undertake a road journey of fifty miles and didn't want anything to impair my ability to drive. He eventually calmed down but I realised then that I would have to smoke the stuff occasionally when it came to twitchy villains, who seemed to need the reassurance that their product is socially acceptable.

Inside the secret world of hash, I found countless layers of characters whose income was wholly derived from the drug. Yet it also became clear that much of the 'vast profit' projected by most law enforcement agencies whenever they try to crack down on hash smuggling is often greatly exaggerated. The phrase 'street value' is a favourite term used by the police after making up a figure of money in order to pat themselves on the back whenever they uncover a large shipment of drugs. That may sound a harsh appraisal but I believe it to be true.

INTRODUCTION

And, finally, then there is the effect of hash itself. One of the wealthiest hash barons I met summed up what the drug meant to him personally when he told me:

I wish I'd never set eyes on a joint, let alone getting involved in the 'business'. Many of us go into it because we think the risks are lower than for coke and smack but the sheer volume of hash means that it is a non-stop conveyor belt and once you are on, it's very hard to get off. My own son got hooked on hash to such an extent that he could barely function. In the end I had to get him committed to a clinic in order to get him off the stuff. In many ways it's more evil than any A-class. It pulls you in gradually and then turns you into an apathetic person, incapable of making a decision. I feel so bad about my kid, especially since it was my involvement in the business that got him smoking hash in the first place. People need to know the true story of hash and the way it reaches their homes. They need to appreciate that it's no better than any of the other stuff.

AUTHOR'S NOTE

Much of the structure of this book relies on a long series of interviews, conversations, and recollections supplied, at times unwittingly, with dozens of individuals over the past two years. Some of the dialogue represented in this book was constructed from available documents, some was drawn from courtroom testimony, and some was reconstituted from the memory of participants.

Obviously, there are few readily available written records covering much of the activities of the criminals involved in the hash business, so I have had to trust the judgement and recollections of numerous individuals, many of whom would rather not have their names reproduced in this book. It has been dependent on the memories of men, fallible, contradictory, touched by pride, and capable of gross omission. But I believe them because there are no hidden agendas in this story and I make no apologies for the strong language, either.

To ensure the accuracy of these stories and anecdotes, I

tried where possible to verify information with more than one source but it was not easy, since paranoia rules when it comes to the underworld and on more than one occasion I was accused of being a 'spy' on behalf of the authorities. So I had to accept the word of many.

I have cross-referenced many incidents with newspaper and TV reports of the same – or similar – crimes and that has helped me fill in many of the holes while at the same time providing the sort of colour and detail which is needed when describing these incidents fully. I have also used Google and newspaper libraries to retell some of the most important other stories involving hash from the past ten years. Some of these accounts are like gold dust to a writer because they enabled me to expand and elaborate in a way that might not have been possible without such important additional details.

Throughout my career as a writer of investigative books about the underworld very few criminals have been unwilling to talk to me once I have met them personally and established a working connection. When I entered the world of hash, I was able to get an introduction to other gangsters and it was as if I was opening a huge door into a secretive world, as more and more criminals contacted me to talk about their involvement with the drug.

I travelled to far-flung, isolated places such as the Rif Mountains of Morocco in my quest for the full story of hash and I was not disappointed. I sometimes spent days on end with only these criminals for company and I learned about their lives outside of crime and how many of them see themselves simply as hard-working individuals, who chanced upon a highly lucrative way to make a living.

I avoided the clichéd, celebrity criminals who've come out in the past to talk about their experiences because the key to this book is that it goes inside a world never previously revealed. I enlisted the help of some ex-criminals and current gangsters in my quest and I remain convinced they were extremely reliable on the whole and I owe them a debt of gratitude for trusting me enough to allow me to hear their most closely guarded secrets.

The way that I linked up with some criminals was truly bizarre. In London, I met a friend of a friend who happened to own property near Tangier and he in turn put me in touch with a Moroccan, who chauffeured him whenever he was in Morocco. This man then contacted a distant cousin who financed a hash farm in the Rif Mountains and that enabled me to make the sort of breakthrough that is essential in my 'business'.

It was a similar story in Britain, Spain and other countries where an assortment of underworld contacts went out of their way to put me in touch with some genuine hash gangsters.

One time I had to meet a Spanish gangster in his hometown of Algeciras in a broken-down, badly lit boathouse. It was impossible to know if I was being set up but I trusted my instincts and, thank goodness, they proved to be right.

In Holland, I met one of Europe's most notorious hash barons on his luxury canal barge in Amsterdam in the heart of one of the main tourist areas.

HASH

Back in Spain, one expat Brit gangster insisted on taking me out on his powerboat because he was paranoid about being spied on by the authorities. The weather was atrocious and the hash baron was snorting lines of cocaine in front of me as he struggled to stop the boat tossing and turning in the storm. In the end he agreed to head back for port. He admitted afterwards he was 'testing' me to see what I was made of. When I didn't complain, he decided he could trust me.

So to all the people I've met during my research who've given me a helping hand, I say, 'Thank you'. Without their input, this book would not have been possible.

The driving motive behind writing this book is to uncover the real story of this shady underworld, which has turned hash into an extraordinarily lucrative business. Sure, there are numerous *smoker's* books out there about the wonders of hash and its emergence as a drug of choice for so many people. But this is the first inside account of hash's hazardous, sometimes even deadly, journey into ordinary people's lives.

Ultimately, I've revealed a story that twists and turns from the mountains of northern Morocco to darkened warehouses overlooking the Mediterranean and beyond, where hash provides a much-needed boost to local economies while also lining the pockets of underworld drug lords. It's been a fascinating journey, which I hope you are going to find as illuminating as I have.

Wensley Clarkson, 2013

PART ONE

MOROCCO – THE KILLING FIELDS WHERE IT ALL BEGINS

Morocco produces more hashish than any other country on earth. Western influence has not only fuelled cannabis cultivation in Morocco, initially through colonialism, it has also steadily pushed up hashish production in the country ever since the onset of the hippy culture in the 1960s.

According to European Union estimates, hash production is Morocco's main source of foreign currency and is a major contributor to the kingdom's gross domestic product.

Some 42 per cent of global hashish production originates in Morocco. The rest of the world's hashish is produced by nearly ninety other countries, including Pakistan (18 per cent), Afghanistan (17 per cent), Lebanon (9 per cent), and India (9 per cent). It is mostly destined for the western and central European markets such as those of the UK, Spain, France, Italy, Portugal, Sweden, Belgium and the Czech Republic. Not surprisingly, most of these markets are dominated primarily by Moroccan hashish.

The cannabis plant first took root in Morocco's Maghreb region in the seventh century AD in the wake of the Arab invasions. However, historians today insist that hash cultivation only began in the fifteenth century. Much later, in the nineteenth century, Sultan Moulay Hassan (King Hassan I) officially authorised cannabis cultivation for local consumption in five douars, or villages, of the Ketama and Beni Khaled tribes, in the Senhaja area of the Rif.

In 1912, the kingdom was split into two protectorates by Spain and France, and the right to cultivate cannabis was granted to a few tribes, this time by Spain. In 1920, local warlord Abdelkrim el-Khattabi unified the Berber tribes of the Rif in their resistance to Spanish authority and set up the independent Republic of the Rif (1921–6), before being defeated by a Franco-Spanish coalition.

Abdelkrim el-Khattabi successfully advocated against 'un-Islamic' cannabis cultivation and consumption during the five years that the independent Republic of the Rif existed. But after 1926 – according to the United Nations Bulletin of Narcotics – the restored Spanish colonials 'set up a zone of toleration to the north of Fez', around the town of Ketama. That zone was gradually reduced until it was officially abolished in 1929, although production continued at a high level.

The French rulers of Morocco tried to ban hash production by royal decree but it wasn't until 1954 that cultivation was completely prohibited in the French protectorate. In 1956, when Morocco gained independence from France, that cannabis prohibition was extended to the former French and Spanish zones.

In 1958, the Berbers rose in rebellion against the government and the uprising was put down by a military expedition composed of two-thirds of the Moroccan army, which, under the command of then-Crown Prince Hassan, even resorted to napalm bombing the Berbers. The civil unrest was partly caused by economic deprivation, since Moroccan Berbers made up the majority of the poorest classes in Morocco. Berber regions had not seen the same development aid as Arabised coastal and urban regions. Eventually it was decided to once again allow cannabis cultivation in the five historical douars of the Ketama and Beni Khaled in order to try and end the conflict in the Rif region.

The town of Ketama – a rural community in the heart of the Al Hoceïma Province of the Taza-Al Hoceima-Taounate region – would eventually become the unofficial hash capital of Morocco. Today it has a population of around 20,000 with an average of ten people per household. Yet behind this poverty lie some of the richest drug barons in the world.

Cannabis cultivation in the Rif expanded greatly in the early 1980s, thanks to ever increasing European demand for hash which had forced the Moroccan cannabis economy to switch from *Kif*, a mixture of chopped marijuana and tobacco, to producing pure hash. Wars in Afghanistan, Lebanon and Syria, plus increased global counter-narcotics efforts had created a gap in the market, enabling Morocco to step in and become the world's number one hash producer.

And as this trade has thrived, so Tangier and the surrounding coastal region evolved into the hash hub of the world. Today, vast hash transactions infuse large amounts of cash into the local economy. At the same time, the recent Algerian civil war next door created a black market in small arms passing through Morocco. This lethal combination of weapons and money sparked intense and violent competition among drug runners in northern Morocco.

Large quantities of Moroccan hash are also sent to West Africa where they are exported through a so-called 'backdoor route' to Europe. Recent seizures of cocaine and hashish packed together in the same manner were made in Morocco and in Spain. Colombian drug traffickers have allied themselves to their Moroccan hash counterparts and either now ship cocaine directly to Morocco, or store it temporarily in West Africa. Some Moroccan hash is also exported to Algeria, via the Oujda–Maghnia road, a notorious route for contraband and people-smuggling.

In more recent years there have been numerous examples of the Moroccan hash barons' power and influence. The drug lords use increasingly complex money laundering schemes involving numerous countries. Many in Morocco believe the drug trade has 'gone industrial', integrating itself into large Moroccan firms in agribusinesses, fishing, transportation and import-export operations. It's the perfect cover for hash smuggling.

One of Morocco's most notorious hash barons – arrested in the mid-1990s – revealed at his trial how his sophisticated and massive organisation had multiple international connections. His gang transported hash out of the central Rif, stockpiled it in the Rif 'border' town of Tetouan, shipped it to Spain by sea where it was then delivered to wholesalers in Amsterdam. In addition to bank accounts in Morocco, Spain, Gibraltar and Canada, along with a yacht and fifteen cars, this particular hash baron boasted of personal, commercial and political ties to the Castro regime in Cuba. He was also in regular contact with the Colombian cocaine cartels, eager to use Morocco's easily penetrable borders as perfect distribution points into Europe.

Today, Morocco's hashish trade is estimated to net $12 billion a year, providing a livelihood to nearly one million people and hash production continues to soar in the Cherifian kingdom, in the heart of the Rif region, where the Berbers' favourite saying is that 'only Kif grows on the land of Ketama'.

According to Dutch and European Union official estimates, cannabis was grown on around 25,000 hectares in the mid-1980s, on 60,000 hectares in 1993, and on 75,000 hectares in 1995 and it's safe to assume it has been rising at that rate ever since. Pollen counts in Southern Spain recently revealed that huge quantities of cannabis pollen were blowing north from the Rif Mountains, 42km across the Straits of Gibraltar and up to 160km inland.

In the mid-1990s, record rainfalls followed drought years, helping the Rif area increase its cultivation of cannabis by another 10 per cent (the average hectare of cannabis produces two to eight tonnes of raw plant). This meant more jobs in the drug trade for those who could find no other work. With the hash trade continuing to grow, areas used for cultivation spread beyond the traditional growing areas of the central Rif to the west and south in provinces including Chefchaouen,

Larache, Taounate and also to the east in the province of Al Hoceima.

The inhabitants of this barren region of Morocco are known as Riffians, a Berber people with their own language called Riffian, athough many speak Moroccan Arabic, Spanish or French as second or third languages. Riffian Berbers are defined as Mediterranean, making these tribes closer to Europeans than to Africans (which explains why so many of the people I encountered in this region had blue eyes and European features).

The Berbers are often portrayed as nomadic peoples crossing the desert on camels. But they also practise sedentary agriculture in the mountains and valleys in this region. Throughout history the Berbers have engaged in trade, which has had a tremendous influence on the history of the African and European continents as they were the first to establish trade routes from as far afield as West Africa to the Mediterranean and have helped connect the peoples of southern Europe with much of sub-Saharan Africa for more than a thousand years. No wonder that many of the Berbers of today provide the backbone for the production of hash demanded by Europe and beyond.

For centuries, the Berbers in these parts cultivated the lowlands in winter and grazed their flocks in mountain meadows during the summer. Others were year-round pastoral nomads. The principal Berber crops then were wheat, barley, fruits, vegetables, nuts and olives. Cattle, sheep and goats were maintained in herds, together with oxen, mules, camels and horses for draft and transportation. But the value of hash has overtaken everything to become the crop of choice for most Berber farmers.

Hash thrives on the Rif region's steep slopes and poor soils, combined with heavy but irregular rainfall compounded by a lack of irrigation infrastructures, making most crops other than cannabis not worth the intense labour they require. Rain-fed cannabis cultivation brings seven to eight times more revenues than barley cultivation.

Today, as they have done for hundreds of years, those same sedentary Berber farmers occupy single-storey stone houses while seasonally nomadic groups erect strongholds of pounded earth for defence and storage and live in goat-hair tents when at pasture. Meanwhile the Berber women – who have a greater degree of personal freedom than females among the traditional Arabs – work at pottery making and weaving. Almost all Berbers are Muslims, but various pre-Islamic religious elements survive among them, chiefly the worship of local saints and the veneration of their tombs.

Berber local governments tend to be more communal and less authoritarian than their Arab counterparts. Yet Berber society can be fragmented with a handful of families making up a clan. Several clans form a community, and many communities make an ethnic group. The simplest Berber political structure, found in villages in the Rif mountains, is the *jama'ah*, a meeting of all reputable adult men in the village square. Fully nomadic groups elect a permanent chieftain and council, while seasonal nomads annually elect a summer chief to direct the migration.

Every now and again the Moroccan government captures a hash shipment to try and demonstrate to US and European authorities that they are serious in their fight against drugs. In 2008, the Moroccan navy seized three tonnes of Europe-bound hashish off the Mediterranean port of Nador. Local politicians suspected that 'raid' was set up through local hash barons, who wanted to help the government look as if they were winning their 'war' against drugs. Moroccan drug lords also suspected that a local terrorist group was trying to muscle in on their hash crop. They were right.

A joint secret service investigation by French and Spanish intelligence officials later established that this shipment of hash together with another hash seizure by the Spanish authorities off the island of Ibiza was an important part of a complex financing network serving the Algeria-based Salafist Group for Preaching and Combat, affiliated since 2005 with al-Qaeda. The group admitted responsibility for two bombings in Algiers that killed thirty people and left 200 injured.

The investigation – by Spain's Centro Nacional de Inteligencia and France's Renseignements Généraux – was first launched after Spanish police found that the Islamists behind the deadly March 2004 bombings in Madrid that claimed 191 lives bought their explosives from former miners based in northern Spain, in return for blocks of hashish.

Meanwhile, Moroccan government officials continue to bridle at open criticism of their 'policy' on hash.

When Moroccan politician Chakib el-Khayari criticised his country's loose anti-drug policy he got three years in prison. Moroccan officials claimed that el-Khayari made his outburst at the request of the Spanish secret services. In response, the Moroccan government closed down two European manned observation posts set up as part of the so-called war on terror. Many believe Moroccan authorities were sending out a clear message to their critics: don't touch our hash, or we'll be less than co-operative in the fight against terrorism.

Hash trafficking from Morocco, it seems, also goes hand in hand with human trafficking. There are many different methods used to smuggle migrants: in cargo boats or fishing boats, but there are also networks in Morocco with contacts within the crews of passenger boats and customs officials who accept unrecorded passengers. In Larache province, the cheapest and most popular method is to cross the Strait of Gibraltar in *pateras*, small five-to-seven-metre fishing boats. These illegal migrants smuggled to Europe are often forced to carry hash to hand over the other side.

In Morocco, few cannabis growers from the Rif have the resources and connections required to ship hashish to Tangier and the other main ports on the Mediterranean coast, let alone across the sea to Spain. Hashish trafficking from the Rif area relies on 'bought' roads and traffickers, not farmers, have the financial and socio-political means to do this.

'Buying the roads' is renowned as an integral part of the Moroccan trafficking and smuggling process. Hash barons often pay for tracks and roads to be built across national and international roadblocks and checkpoints. They look on it as purchasing the transit of their cargo, no matter what that cargo consists of. Both legal and illegal goods can be traded on the same routes or even together in the same shipment.

So the mountaineous Rif region's reputation as a 'country within a country' is clearly defined. It's a dangerous place where the law of the gun rules above all else. But it is the obvious first step in uncovering the truth about hash.

CHAPTER 1

THE SECRET KINGDOM OF 'KIF'

My journey into the hash badlands of Morocco's Rif Mountain region began with a meeting in a fashionable pub in London's trendy King's Road with a former cannabis smuggler called Si, who still owned property in Morocco and had promised he could get me access to one of the secretive, isolated mountain-top hash farms that dominate the Rif region.

Si immediately warned me that it would not be easy. 'They'll think you're planning to try and set up a hash deal. They're Berber people and they don't trust strangers,' said Si. 'It's a closed society, mate. That's why it's survived all these hundreds and thousands of years. They don't like foreigners sticking their noses in their business.'

Eventually Si pulled his mobile out of his pocket and punched out a number. Speaking in rapid fire French he told the person at the other end of the line my name and that I was a writer. Then he handed the phone to me. 'His name is Leff and he speaks good English.'

It turned out Leff was speaking to me from Tangier and his cousin, he said, 'knew of' a hash farm in the mountains overlooking the so-called hash capital of Ketama, where the drug ruled every aspect of local life. It was also a place that foreign criminals and even tourists had ventured – and never returned. Leff sounded friendly enough and said with remarkable coolness and ease that he could set the whole visit up for me – for a price.

I explained that my budget was non-existent. Surprisingly, Leff agreed to my terms without any argument. I had expected a long bartering session. After making an arrangement to meet him in Tangier the following week, I put the phone down and asked Si why Leff was helping me. 'Because he owes me a big favour. That's why.'

Si never told me what had happened between them and I decided from the tone of his voice it was best not to ask. The following day Si called me and said he had a 'business meeting' in Morocco the following week, so he'd accompany me on my trip into the Rif Mountains. I was relieved to have him along for the ride.

Five days later I arrived with Si in the bustling port city of Tangier on a ferry from the Spanish mainland. We met Leff and his 'cousin' Fara in a cafe and discussed the arrangements. They promptly disappeared after promising to meet us in Ketama forty-eight hours later. Si assured me they would turn up. It all seemed too easy at this stage but clearly having Si on board was my passport into Morocco's secret world of hash.

The following morning we headed east out of Tangier in a rented four-by-four along the Mediterranean coast and then turned south towards the Rif Mountains. Gradually, the influences of hash became obvious: heavily guarded villas with strangely stylised pagodas and expensive German cars in the driveways plus a seemingly endless supply of young men drifting along the main roads – and we hadn't even got into the Rif region yet.

Many are said to fear that Morocco is under threat from an Islamist challenge to its stability and that international drug trafficking is relentlessly chipping away at the state's power and influence. But from where I sat that day it looked as if Morocco's drug networks were also aiding financial stability. The hash barons are rich and wealthy and, in Morocco, money buys you everything. Many even reckon the drug barons and the strict Islamists in the north draw upon the same group of discontented poor, creating possible alliances and the sharing of resources and tactics. No wonder many people say these two groups hold the majority of power in these parts.

One Berber hash baron called H'midou Dib still retains folk hero status in the Rif region. A former fisherman, he constructed his own port in Sidi Kankouch on the coast north of Tangier, which was an embarkation point for a steady stream of high-speed inflatables on their way to

Europe with hash shipments. Dib developed an enormous network of loyal foot soldiers and villagers eager to protect him. He supplied jobs, built mosques, delivered social services and kept the despised authorities at bay. Dib was also involved in complex real estate transactions in Tangier, money laundering operations and other elements of organised crime. Through sheer wealth and organisation, he was one of a handful of criminals who'd become leaders of that quasi-state in the Rif region. Even the Moroccan government itself admits that Ketama and the surrounding Rif region enjoys 'semi-independence' from the rest of the country. Surrounded by mountains with peaks reaching heights of almost 3,000 metres, it has been a smugglers' paradise for centuries.

As we drove up the potholed, winding, deserted blacktop towards Ketama, I noticed a police car in my rear mirror. Within five minutes, we'd been stopped and the car searched and Si had suggested I hand over a 20 dirham note to the two friendly officers, who then wished us well on our journey. 'Look out for the bad men,' said one of them, laughing as he slid his finger across his own throat.

From here onwards, the countryside turned steep and rugged. It was clear we were now in no-man's land, a place where few strangers dared to tread. 'I bet those cops'll be telling all their mates in Ketama that we're on our way into town,' said Si. 'That police roadblock marked the end of Moroccan rule. We're now in bandit country, my friend.'

*

The early golden sun rises over Ketama. The earth-red rooftops glow in the morning light. Prayers are being called as the city wakes. The hypnotic sound of a muezzin wailing through loudspeakers casts an eerie atmosphere.

Ketama's status is perfectly summed up by the absence of Moroccan police, as well as of Moroccan flags on any house or building. You get the impression these people look after themselves and don't appreciate any interference – but then the main produce of the region is hash, so it's not that surprising.

This gateway to the hash frontier is notoriously – and many say deliberately – badly connected to other urban centres of Morocco by winding, treacherous mountain roads, which help it thrive as a base for the illicit production and sale of what locals call *Kif*, an Arabic word meaning 'perfect bliss'.

In Ketama, you instantly get the feeling that local people are sizing up all newcomers. They are up early in these parts. The cafes are bustling with men, most of whom earn their living from the cultivation of cannabis.

Some are smoking Kif. Nearly all are watching the early TV news on Al-Jazeera. It's the middle of the Arab Spring in early 2011. Uprisings across the Arab world are all that anyone seems to be talking about.

There were fears within the Moroccan authorities that the neighbouring anarchy might spread into this nation. As a result, two army tanks are positioned just outside Ketama's main square as a 'warning' to anyone who might decide that

Morocco should get caught up in the biggest revolution to hit the Arab world in centuries. But Ketama's Berber population don't even acknowledge the tanks because they know the army will not stop them going about their daily business, dealing in hash.

The men up early in the cafes that morning seem to be no more than vaguely curious about what their Arab neighbours are doing. There is a feeling of contentment among many more Moroccans than in most other North African nations. A local man we met called Omar explained: 'In Morocco we like to feel we have a good life, even though most of us have little money. The King respects his people. The politicians are not extreme or brutal. We trust the government.'

Or maybe the government is simply happy to let hash rule the economy of this rugged region?

'The people of the Rif Mountains know that so long as they can support themselves then the rest of Morocco will leave them alone,' adds Omar.

If the government and police tried to crack down in this region they'd have a mini-revolution on their hands. As Omar explains: 'We are the authority in these parts. We run ourselves. The Kif goes in and out without restrictions. It is the lifeblood of this region. Without it there would be poverty and starvation. Why would the government want to change that?'

There is a lot of wise logic behind Omar's explanation. It would take a small army of Moroccan soldiers many years to eradicate the cannabis crop in the way that the United States would wish to happen. 'What's the point?' says Omar. 'The Kif provides us with money, happiness, homes and contentment. The King and his government knows this only too well. It's been like this for thousands of years and it's never going to change as long as the West wants our Kif.'

In the muddy, uneven main street of Ketama, huge tractors from local farms are parked alongside gleaming flatbed trucks, Mercedes and BMW saloons. This is the proof that hash provides untold riches to some of the people who live in these parts.

Inside one cafe, I smell the familiar whiff of Kif from within a group of middle-aged men sitting close to the over-hanging TV set as it blares out the latest news on the Arab uprising. They glance menacingly at myself and Si. We look away, careful not to catch their stares for too long as it could spark trouble. 'Just keep yer eyes off them and they'll leave us alone,' says Si.

Overhanging the bar area are two huge sheep carcasses, which will be sliced up and cooked on a massive concrete barbecue outside later that day. The coffee is bitter and thick, almost like syrup.

Opposite us, two old men look up and examine us closely before going back to their conversation. I start to wonder why we've made ourselves so conspicuous in this hash town ahead of the trip up into the lawless mountains that overlook it. But Leff and Fara from Tangier had insisted we meet at this particular cafe. It's almost like a test for us. It feels as if we are being examined before being allowed to enter the secret kingdom of Kif.

Si is a vital lynchpin. He knows these parts well. As he explains: 'This place is a shithole once you look beyond the Beemers and Mercs. Many of the locals say that strangers who turn up here don't usually stay for long. I've seen men shot at in the main street here. It's a dog eat dog kind of place.'

We're just finishing up our bittersweet coffees when Si's mobile rings. It's Leff, the hash farm fixer. He and his cousin Fara have changed the plan and now want us to meet them at the hash farm. Si talks to Leff in razor-fast French. 'They're worried about being seen with us in Ketama,' he says. Then he announces it is time to leave.

We walk out of the cafe and head to our rented red Toyota Land Cruiser slung up outside the cafe. Three kids have gathered round it. One of them asks, somewhat threateningly, for some money. Si asks me for five dirhams and I give it to him to hand to the boy.

'If you don't pay 'em they'll get their big brothers to slash our tyres next time we're in town,' explains Si.

Si then takes the wheel and we set off through bustling Ketama. Si chats to locals in perfect Arabic and French as we sit in slow traffic in the crowded main street. Then, for the first time, Si reveals he learned the languages while serving four years in a Moroccan jail for smuggling hash.

Si has been out for six years, and now lives half the year near Murcia, in Spain, and the other half in London. He got into drug smuggling because his brother was a renowned hash baron who also lived in Spain after absconding from a five-year prison sentence in the UK. Britain was unable to extradite him due to a legal technicality, but he paid the ultimate price for crossing a Moroccan drug baron when he was shot dead in a warehouse on the Costa del Sol. His body was then dumped inside his own Range Rover at a local airport car park. 'That was a message to others not to cross this Moroccan. Hash is a nasty old business,' explains Si, who even managed to sound matter-of-fact when discussing the murder of his own sibling.

Si says he took over his brother's hash connections, although he claims that these days he is virtually retired after making enough cash to live comfortably for the rest of his life.

As we finally leave the traffic and staring people behind to begin the steep drive up towards the mountain peaks, Si continues to explain his life backstory. 'I was nicking cars and stuff from the age of twelve. It was the only way to survive where I came from. I looked up to my brother then. He seemed to have it all. By the time he was twenty-one, he was driving a flash car and making a fortune from coke and weed. But then he got nicked and one of Manchester's biggest firms decided he was a liability, so he fucked off to Spain and began all over again in the hash game. He had the bottle to deal directly with the Moroccans and the police back home couldn't get him back because of a legal technicality, which had allowed him to get bail when he was still in Manchester.'

Si interrupts himself to point over the edge of the road as we climb the side of a mountain. 'There's a few of my mates down there somewhere,' he says, almost casually. 'They got too heavily involved with the local hash boys and ended up in shallow graves.'

We continue our journey along hazardous, rocky tracks. Tarmac roads simply don't exist in these parts. Si tells me that most of the roads have been carved out of the mountainside by the drug barons, who wanted quick routes away from the hash farms, so they can transport hash swiftly and safely out of the Rif Mountains. Until twenty years ago, many of these tracks did not exist and smugglers often transported hash by donkey through a mountain pass from one isolated hash farm down to the nearest coastal port.

'If you want a road out here, then you pay for it yourself and make sure that only your friends use it,' explains Si.

The full impact of what he says only comes home to me as we slow down to stop in front of a makeshift gate, a plank of wood leaning on a rusting oil drum slung across the mountain-edge track. Before Si has even pulled up the handbrake of the Land Cruiser, two wiry-looking locals appear from behind a huge boulder.

Slung over each of their shoulders are Uzi machine guns. Yet they are smiling as they approach our vehicle.

'Fuck,' says Si. 'Sit tight. I'll sort this out.'

Si jumps out of the car and greets the men. They seem deeply suspicious and look at him through narrowing eyes. One of them has a scar across his left cheek.

Then Si shoves the man with the scar in the shoulder. The local looks furious for a split second before a further, breathless exchange of words. This is followed by a broad grin across scar-man's face. I open the window to try and hear what they are saying. Si turns and shouts at me.

'I know this bastard from prison. Small world, eh?'

Si then goes into a huddle with the man as his friend joins them. After a few moments, Si emerges and shouts across at me.

'You got 500 dirhams?'

I don't argue and hand it to Si through the open window.

He screws the note up in his hand and throws it playfully at the local, who catches it and laughs. Si and the man hug warmly and we are on our way.

It's only as Si crunches the Land Cruiser into third gear up the winding track two or three minutes later that he says anything.

'Guess how he got that scar.'

'I haven't a clue.'

'He tried slashing me with a razor blade in the prison canteen and I turned it back on him.'

'Right.'

'That's how you make mates inside a Moroccan jail.'

'How much further d'you reckon?' I ask Si, changing the subject.

'I think it's straight up this road,' says Si. 'They said you can't miss it.'

Twenty minutes later and we are so high up the side of a

mountain that the clouds are drifting across the track, making driving even more hazardous. Occasionally through the mist we spot tiny matchstick figures of men and women working the fields in the distance.

'They'll be phoning the farmers on their mobiles saying there are strangers around,' says Si as casual as ever. 'Nothing moves round these parts without everyone knowing about it.'

As the mid-morning sun begins to burn away the cloud cover, the peaks of three snow-capped mountains come into full view ahead of us. We turn a sharp left around a mountain pass between two huge boulders and hundreds of feet high above us to the left is a tiny concrete shack. I can just make out the figure of a man sitting outside the building smoking.

'That's gotta be the place,' says Si.

'How do we get up there?' I ask.

'You walk, old son,' said Si. 'Nothing's easy round these parts.'

Just then the man up in the distance waves in our direction. It's a relief to know he is even expecting us.

Ten minutes later we've reached the shack after a twisting and turning hike up a steep rocky verge. It's a strange feeling to know people must have been talking about your arrival before you've even got there.

Then, as if he is reading my mind, Si explains: 'The maximum we should stay here is a couple of hours before everyone knows we're around. Then we might have a few problems.'

'Why?'

'Because every fucker within a hundred miles of here will want paying. That's why.'

'What happens if we don't pay them?'

'They nick our watches and our phones and our wallets, if we're lucky.'

The man we saw from below is smoking as we approach his building. He looks very young, maybe no more than about twenty or twenty-one. He seems friendly enough but then he has just finished smoking a big Kif spliff while awaiting our arrival. The red polka-dot neckerchief around his neck contrasts oddly with the tatty jeans, sweat-soaked T-shirt and flip-flops.

Just then I catch a glimpse of a striking Moroccan woman of about the same age as the man and a small child, probably no more than two years old. They're sitting outside the back area of the shack by a makeshift clothesline. The man seems irritated they've come into view and immediately shouts at them. They disappear inside.

'For fuck's sake don't look at his wife. He'll take it as an insult,' explains Si, helpfully.

The man turns and glances at us through narrow, suspicious, bright-blue eyes. He must be a Berber because he looks more European than Arab.

Si engages the man in a proper conversation while I retreat to sit on a rock in front of the shack.

Si eventually beckons to me to follow him and the man inside the shack. Si explains that we can watch him sieving a crop of cannabis buds. It's only then I am formally introduced to the man, whose name is Hassan.

Later, I discover that Hassan keeps a gun under the bed he shares with his wife, just in case his friends turn into his enemies.

CHAPTER 2

HASSAN

The nondescript scrubland behind Hassan's house is where bushels of cannabis, left to dry in the hot sun, are hanging from wooden frames. In this climate very little grows apart from cannabis and Hassan depends on this crop to support his family. Inside the shack, Si translates as Hassan explains the process of how the hashish is made as he places the cannabis buds on a giant sieve and covers it with a tarpaulin.

Hassan then beats the tarpaulin with sticks rather like a drum. The pollen or resin crystals – which contain the drug's main psychoactive ingredient THC – break from the plant and fall through the sieve. When the drumming is complete, Hassan gathers the pollen together, compressing it to form bricks of yellowy-brown hash.

As Hassan prepares the hash, he talks about his family, who've been harvesting hash for three generations. He tells of his dream of one day leaving the mountains and seeking his fortune in Europe. It seems strange to hear this young man talking about his future when we are sitting thousands of feet up in one of the world's most isolated mountain ranges.

Even more confusing is Hassan's appearance. With his piercing pale blue eyes and thick brown curly hair, he looks very European. His granite shaped face and lean physique would not look out of place on the catwalk of a London fashion show. It seems incongruous that he has a wife and child tucked away in a backroom just a few feet from where we are talking.

As Hassan starts to relax more in our company he opens up about his lonely life on top of the mountain. 'There is no other job for me here. My father and grandfather harvested Kif and it is the way to survive out here. I know that others are making much more money from it than me but that is the way it goes out here. We farmers are just the start of the supply chain. We have little power to force the gangsters to pay more for the Kif because there is so much of it here they will simply go and buy it elsewhere.'

Hassan shrugs his shoulders a lot, giving the impression that despite his earlier claim to want a better life in Europe, he knows in his heart of hearts that he will probably end up harvesting cannabis for the rest of his working life. After showing us the process, he sits down with Si and the two men enjoy a massive spliff together and that's when Hassan really starts to open up.

'I have worked and lived up here since I was fourteen.

28

School was pretty much a waste of time because round these parts you know the only job you can hope for is to harvest Kif and that doesn't require qualifications and exams. Sure, it's lonely up here and in the winter it's bitterly cold but it was much more lonely before I got married. Having a wife is my salvation in many ways. It is the key to my survival.'

But, I ask through Si, what are the dangers associated with producing Kif in the world's hashish capital? Hassan hesitates and whispers a few words to Si, who explains: 'He is worried about upsetting the middlemen. He thinks you will get him into trouble.'

I try to reassure Hassan, through Si, by promising to use a different name for him in my book and assuring him I will not reveal the specific location of his hash farm. He nods somewhat reluctantly and then lowers his voice.

'You see, the men who buy the Kif from me and then smuggle it into Europe are often bad people. They treat us farmers like shit but what choice do we have? I now keep a gun under my bed because there have been many bad incidents in the past.'

Hassan explains that one hash gangster accused him of watering down the Kif with powdered tree bark and earth. 'This guy came up here with three others in the middle of the night, dragged me out of my bed and then threatened to rape my wife at gunpoint. If I had had my gun then I would have tried to shoot them all dead. They then forced me to give them another shipment of Kif for free to replace the stuff they said I had watered down. I had to do it to stop them hurting my wife.'

It's not clear from what Hassan is saying as to whether he still does business with the same men who threatened to rape his wife. But he makes a point of telling this story in a quiet, conspiratorial tone that leaves one with the distinct impression he does.

Hassan says he earns about £2,000 a year from harvesting Kif. He knows others are making a hundred times that amount out of his same crop. 'Sometimes I think about defying the gangsters and selling my own Kif in Ketama but the criminals would soon find out and I'd be killed.' There are strict demarcation lines in the Rif region when it comes to the production of hash. People who step out of line and try to set up their own 'business' in defiance of the local drug lords don't tend to enjoy long and healthy lives.

Hassan explains: 'I had an uncle once who used to harvest Kif on his own plot of land. He got fed up with being forced to sell for low prices, so he decided to cut out the middleman and headed down into Ketama to try and find a buyer direct. My father told me that my uncle lasted all of two days in Ketama before his body was found dumped in an alleyway behind one of the town's most popular cafes. It was a message to others not to try and ignore the Kif gangsters.'

Hassan says he fears the day when his daughter is old enough to attend the local school in Ketama because there have been a number of kidnappings of children from the school after their fathers fell out with local drug lords. 'In many ways,' says Hassan, 'it's safer to keep my daughter out of school completely. The trouble is that it is a vicious circle because if she gets no education then she will never have a chance to leave this place and I want her to experience the world away from here and be happy and successful.'

Just then Hassan is diverted by a small cloud of dust off in the distance on the same mountainside track we had driven up a moment ago. We can just make out a flatbed truck travelling at what appears to be high speed. We all glance down as a much bigger lorry appears from around a corner coming in the opposite direction. The two vehicles are about two hundred feet apart but neither seems to be slowing down to give way.

Hassan says nothing but continues watching the scene down below intently. The lorry is forced to the edge of the track where there is a drop of at least 500 feet. The smaller vehicle surges past the lorry hooting its horn loudly but not even slowing down to acknowledge the existence of the other, much bigger vehicle.

'Okay,' says Hassan. 'I must be careful what I say from now on. The men from Tangier are here.'

Down below us, the Moroccans Leff and Fara, whom I met through Si in Tangier two days earlier, jump out of a gleaming $35,000 Nissan flatbed truck. A strong wind is starting to blow in from the east and an uneasy feeling is suddenly in the air.

CHAPTER 3

LEFF AND FARA

It soon emerges that Leff and his associate Fara have a part-share in Hassan's hash farm and they immediately make it clear who's in charge as they check the 'produce', which lies in sacks outside the front of the shack. Fara's backstory is chilling and disturbing. He was first recruited into the 'business' as a thirteen-year-old street hustler in Tangier by an older man who sexually abused him. He ended up killing the man and taking over his hash connections. No one objected because the older man had a reputation as a sexual predator, so many were happy to see the end of him, according to Leff.

Leff is Fara's cousin and that's how he got involved in the hash trade. He explains: 'It's like the Wild West out here but there is such great demand for hash in Tangier and Europe that it made sense to put some money into Hassan's farm and begin a proper production line.'

I'm already beginning to suspect that Leff and Fara wouldn't hesitate to intimidate Hassan, especially since Hassan shrinks very much into the background following the arrival of the two Tangier gangsters.

Fara seems much more edgy than when we first met in Tangier. He even complains about my presence to both Si and Leff, despite having agreed everything two days earlier. 'He is worried because we make it a rule never to allow other people up here in case they tell criminals about our business,' says Leff. Si and I try to reassure him we have no intention of doing that.

Then Leff shrugs his shoulders. 'I told Fara it's good for people out there who smoke to understand how difficult it is to get them their hash. It's not an easy business. The Kif is handled by many people before it gets to places like London. Sometimes I think the people who smoke it over there think it gets picked up from the mountainside and driven straight to Piccadilly Circus. If only . . .'

Leff is eloquent and confident and reveals that he is university educated. He even spent a year in London learning English at a language school in Fulham, west London. 'I wish I was there now. I love London. One day I hope to have enough money to buy myself a work permit and settle over there with a beautiful English girl.' It's such a pat reply I presume he must be telling the truth.

But, I ask Leff, how does a well-educated, middle-class Tangier resident end up working in the underworld as a hash dealer? 'It's simple. The money is fucking good, my friend,' he says. 'I went to school with Fara when we were just ten years old. He left at fourteen and then had some problems but he's turned his life around now. When I met him again I was twenty-one, just out of university with a degree but there were no jobs in Tangier. Fara had a BMW and a rich life. I had nothing. When he asked me if I wanted to work with him, I jumped at the chance.'

Fara appeared at the doorway to Hassan's shack and barked some orders in Arabic to Leff. 'He's still suspicious of you. He keeps saying he thinks you're working for the police.' Then Leff slapped my thigh playfully and added: 'Only joking!'

But it was clear after I learned about Fara's disturbing past that he was the trigger-happy one of the pair. He constantly seemed on edge and Leff spent much of his time calming his partner down. 'Fara says I bring him back down to earth. He needs me with him otherwise he would lose his temper and end up dead.' Leff laughed again but I suspected he was telling the truth.

I then ask about their families back in Tangier. What do they think about their 'career'? Leff smiles yet again: 'They know what I do and they're cool with it because Kif is an important industry for the Moroccan economy. In any case a lot of people in Tangier smoke hash. It's no big deal.'

Just then Fara sits down on a big stone outside the shack and lights up a massive spliff, takes three huge sucks on it and then passes it to Leff, saying something in Arabic.

It's just become apparent that both Leff and Fara have one

classic weakness. They adore smoking hash. Surely that breaks the golden rule for any professional criminals involved with the drug?

'It's not a problem,' Leff says with a shrug. 'We both love to smoke but we make sure it doesn't affect our ability to make money from Kif.'

The effect of the hash seems to calm both Fara and Leff down and they drift effortlessly from hard-nosed criminals into slightly vulnerable-looking young Moroccan men, who obviously find hash the best way to try and forget their problems.

Hassan the farmer, meanwhile, is now back inside the shack going through the final stages of the process to produce more hash for the middlemen. He is pouring it into ten-kilo sacks. Hassan delivers yet another sack outside to the now vacant looking Fara, who opens it and smells it like Hannibal Lector inhaling a fava bean stew. Fara looks up, grins broadly and passes the bag to Leff, who performs a similar task before tying up the bag and casually leaving it on the ground.

It's only then I enquire about the value of such a bag. Leff says in English: 'That's worth maybe $100,000 in Europe.' Then he laughs. 'But we make sure that Hassan doesn't realise it!'

Over the following half an hour, Fara and Leff load the bags onto the back of the flatbed truck below before announcing they will meet us back in Ketama, at the base of the vast valley. We all agree it would be 'indiscreet' if they were seen in a convoy with our vehicle.

Si – who himself had sucked on a couple of joints over the previous half an hour – merrily acts as intermediary. He even adds: 'They're right. A convoy filled with strangers could really wind up the locals.'

Just before departing, Hassan reappears from inside the shack and talks to me through Si. 'He wants to know how much Kif costs in the UK.' There is an awkward wall of silence as it becomes clear that Fara and Leff are listening to this exchange. Fara butts in and screams something in Arabic at Hassan. Si translates: 'He's just told Hassan to mind his own fucking business.'

Hassan does yet another of his customary shrugging of the shoulders and tries to laugh it off. But then Fara yells even more angrily at Hassan. Hassan shouts back and for a moment the two men have a face-off as they try to stare each other down. Eventually, Leff intercedes and laughs while he tells them both to calm down.

As Fara walks off down the hill towards his truck with the last bag of Kif, he looks up at Hassan, still standing outside his shack with his arms folded, glaring at the other man with a snarling expression on his face.

Minutes later we set off ahead of the flatbed so as not to be seen driving in convoy to Ketama. I turned and looked behind me to see Fara still glaring up at Hassan in the distance.

That's when I decided that Fara must have been the same man who'd threatened to rape Hassan's wife.

*

It's now mid-afternoon in Ketama and there is no sign of Fara or Leff in a dusty layby on the edge of town, where we had arranged to meet them. After more than half an hour of waiting, Si walks me to the nearby souk, which is awash with dozens of traders, all pushing to sell their wares, from food to silk. Within this general market place, Si takes me to a discreet shop, where he's quickly ushered inside. Here you can buy a 'Caramelo' or 'egg', which is a small pre-packed amount of hash, wrapped in clingfilm. Amateur smugglers can buy it, swallow it, and then travel over the border en route to Europe. People tend to buy between five and fifty at any one time. Si gives me a chilling first-hand account of how he met such Westerners in jail.

'They're fuckin' stupid because the clingfilm is paper-thin and there is a danger it can burst inside you and then you're in real trouble,' explains Si. 'I knew one guy who came here twice from Newcastle. He bought four dozen packs and then swallowed the lot with a bottle of castor oil to help them slip down more easily. First time he did it was a doddle but when he came back he got greedy and swallowed even more packs and, surprise, surprise, two of them burst as he got off the plane the other end. He was lucky there was a doctor at the airport but he ended up serving three years for smuggling. Stupid bastard, eh?'

Just then Leff finally calls me from his mobile. As he speaks, I can tell he's stoned because he keeps laughing and there is the sound of his associate Fara doing likewise in the background. They are clearly off their heads and I can just make out from Leff that they are in a cafe halfway down the mountainside. I'm irritated because I have to be back in Tangier as quickly as possible to catch a ferry to Algeciras in Spain, where I have an appointment with a Costa del Sol hash baron that very same evening.

I know that Leff is fishing for a 'fee' from me, even though I told him I could not afford to pay anything for their help. Suddenly, the friendly potted-out voice changes tone.

'You must wait for us,' says Leff. 'Or there may be problems. We need to discuss the expenses.'

I didn't like the coldness in his voice so I ignored his comment about money and told Leff I would wait for him but he must hurry up. Keeping Leff calm seemed a sensible move.

Si doesn't sound in the least bit surprised when I explain what has happened. 'Sounds like it's the devil or the deep blue sea, mate.'

I then remembered an anecdote Leff had told me just a few hours earlier up in the mountains about how he and Fara had to shoot a man in the leg as a warning to a rival gang not to invade their hash farm.

'Yes, but what's the point in waiting for them?' I ask Si.

'It's up to you, old son. I told them not to fuck us around and now the silly bastards have got off their heads.'

'But Leff is your contact,' I asked. 'I don't want to upset him for that reason.'

'Bollocks,' says Si. 'I haven't done business with those two clowns in years. Let's just fuck off.'

So we opt for the Straits of Gibraltar and head off at high speed in the Land Cruiser for the port of Tangier, three hours west of Ketama. Within an hour of setting off, a call from Leff comes through on my mobile. I look at the screen and listen to it ringing but decide not to answer.

Si laughs alongside me as we pick up speed on the first stretch of dual carriageway we have seen for more than a hundred miles. 'Typical, greedy bastards,' he says. 'Serves 'em right. You know what they say? Don't get high on your own supply.'

I listen to the message from Leff on my phone.

'You motherfucker English asshole. We want money and if we don't get it we will shoot your fuckin' balls off. D'you understand? I will come and find you in London and rape your wife and kidnap your children if you do not pay us. I will call back in ten minutes. If you do not pick up the phone you are a dead man.'

The phone rings exactly ten minutes later. This time I pick it up and then switch it off immediately. I know full well we are probably two hours ahead of this hapless pair of Tangier dopehead gangsters.

Then Si announces: 'They know we're catching a ferry.'

'Good point.'

'Hope it leaves on time.'

The next time I switch on the phone again is when the ferry is pulling away from the port-side of Tangier's newly built passenger terminal, as it sets sail for Algeciras. There are twenty-three messages from Leff awaiting my attention. Most of them feature threats to kill my wife, children, mother, father and promising to 'hunt' me down in London and throw my body in the River Thames. Sitting in the ship's restaurant, Si listens to the messages with a broad grin on his face.

'They fucked up. Not us. Leff will calm down. I'll talk to him in a few days.'

Just then I look out of the porthole and notice a familiar looking flatbed truck travelling at high speed across the deserted car park in front of the ferry disembarkation spot. It screeches to a halt. I can just make out Leff and Fara jumping out and running to the water's edge as the ferry steams slowly between the gap in the harbour wall while making its way out into the Strait of Gibraltar.

'Stupid little bastards,' says Si, drily. 'They'll calm down eventually. The one thing I learned about Moroccans when I was in jail was that they don't hold grudges. In the end they'll respect us for doing a runner. They've only got themselves to blame, haven't they?'

I was tempted to ask Si whether he thought their threats to visit London and my family were serious but decided not to tempt fate.

As the ferry made its way slowly across one of the world's busiest shipping lanes, I flipped open my research notebook and began reading up on my next interviewee – a shadowy character called Zaid.

PART TWO

SPAIN – THE HASH FRONTIER

The market for hash continues to grow in Europe, where it's reckoned that one in five adults have used marijuana or hashish. The European Union's drug agency produced a 700-page report on the use and abuse of cannabis and established that more than 13 million hash smokers use the drug every month in Europe.

Just across a 7.7 nautical mile stretch of water from Morocco lies Spain, which has a hash consumption epidemic on its hands. The Spanish make more seizures of the drug than all other European countries put together but nothing, it seems, can stem the tide of hash flowing across the Strait of Gibraltar from Morocco.

Vast shipments arrive from North Africa virtually every day and the traffickers are always coming up with new methods of smuggling. One of the latest techniques is for gangs to drop loads of hash fitted with radio-transmitting buoys into the Atlantic and have boats pick up the drugs.

In 2012, Spanish police arrested five members of a gang of drug traffickers on the Costa del Sol when 1,600 kilos of hashish was discovered in a house in an operation called 'Sarco'. The investigation started at the end of the previous year when the police became aware of the group and started to identify its members. It was later alleged that the gang of several nationalities moved hash from Spain to Holland, Great Britain and Ireland.

In 2011, 840 kilos of hashish was intercepted on a yacht that had arrived in the port of Marbella from Morocco. The drug was disguised inside twenty-seven bales hidden between the cabin and different parts of the leisure craft. The raid was the culmination of a six-month investigation into the activities of a group of Spanish hash smugglers initially detected on the Costa del Sol. The gang transferred the drugs on the high seas and brought it ashore on different parts of the Málaga coastline. At the beginning of 2011, the group tried to acquire a powerful boat with high top speeds from the Spanish town of La Linea opposite Gibraltar, but the illicit operation failed after the boat was stopped two days after the sale for not having a licence.

Also in Marbella, two French citizens, a father-and-son hash trafficking 'team' were arrested in 2011. Fifty-two kilograms of hashish and €58,340 in cash plus false documents were recovered. The hash was found in a suitcase hidden under a staircase in a house rented by the two men.

A former councillor in the city of Ceuta, a Spanish territory that borders with Morocco, was arrested with 690 kilos of hash in a van he was driving as he was about to board a ferry to Algeciras in 2011. Police – who'd been tipped off – immediately searched his vehicle and located blocks of the drug, hidden in different parts of the vehicle.

The routes of entry of Moroccan hash into Spain are constantly changing due to the use of fast boats with longer ranges. Drug smugglers now reach Spanish provinces such as Huelva, Almería, Murcia and Valencia, where the number of seizures have multiplied in recent years. Large quantities have even been seized as far north as the Ebro river delta.

According to the Observatoire Français des Drogues et des Toxicomanies, Moroccan hash is also sent southward by truck to the Atlantic port of Agadir, to Casablanca and Essaouira, from where much of it is exported through northern Spain. But the favourite route remains smuggling hash in trucks and cars travelling on ferries leaving from the Moroccan Spanish enclaves of Ceuta and Melilla or from the port of Tangier.

Before Spain's current crippling recession, it enjoyed a spectacular ten-year building boom, much of which was driven by 'dirty (black) money' spent by the hash barons. Criminals capitalised on the gold rush mentality that infected Spain in the 1990s and early part of the new century. House prices doubled in the ten years between 1997 and 2007. Unscrupulous local authorities even turned a blind eye to 'front' companies set up by gangsters and took backhanders to grant building licences.

Keen to hide the spoils from hash and other drug smuggling, as well as prostitution, extortion and human trafficking, gangsters channelled hundreds of millions into buying property. Meanwhile, police and judicial authorities were often overwhelmed by the scale and sophistication of criminal activities. On Spain's Costa del Sol – where estate agents believed during the boom years they virtually had a licence to print money – anti-corruption magistrates found themselves dealing with scores of cases.

Just how much 'dirty money' entered Spain in the so-called

boom years is impossible to say. But it is claimed that 40 per cent of all the €500 bills in existence are circulating in Spain. They are called 'Bin Ladens' because, like the terrorist who was the world's most wanted man until his death, everyone knows what they look like but few people have ever actually seen one. These €500 bills fill the envelopes in 'black money' property deals.

Southern Spain was clearly awash with hash and my next subject, Zaid, was one of the biggest names in the business.

CHAPTER 4

ZAID

With Leff and Fara left far behind still fuming in Tangier, it was time to meet an altogether different character. Spanish-born hash baron Zaid was brought up in the port of Algeciras, which itself is only separated from Morocco by the Strait of Gibraltar. Zaid owns and runs a number of warehouses in the industrial area of the city.

After disembarking the ferry from Morocco, Si headed off to his Spanish home in Murcia, while I was met by Paco, one of Zaid's men. We drive off in his car for a night-time rendezvous with the man himself. Although Paco speaks no English, I speak enough Spanish to manage a light conversation, which is punctuated by awkward silences as the vehicle heads through the rundown suburbs of Algeciras. As we near an industrial area, Paco drives around and around the same block of warehouses at least five times. He helpfully explains that this is done in order to make sure the police are not tailing him because he does not want to lead them to Zaid's headquarters.

Eventually Paco parks the car and as a secondary safety measure we walk at least a quarter of a mile to a warehouse. The streets are badly lit and every time a car passes us, Paco carefully checks it out with a squint of his eyes.

Eventually we reach a big garage-type door with a smaller door built within it. Paco knocks twice. We enter to find ourselves in a warehouse about four times the size of a normal lock-up garage with an office attached to it. Five men are gathered around a small white Citroën with its rear tailgate open. The men glance up with menacing looks on their faces until they recognise Paco. One of the men turns and approaches us and introduces himself as Zaid. He's short and stocky and walks like a weightlifter on steroids. He talks in quickfire Spanish that is quite hard for me to understand.

Zaid has only agreed to meet me because he is the brother-in-law of a lawyer I know in Málaga. Without this introduction, he tells me, he wouldn't come near me. He considers journalists – *Periodistas* – to be 'the enemy'. He immediately tells me how the newspapers exaggerate stories about drugs, which in turn then puts more pressure on Spain's Policia National and Guardia Civil to arrest hash barons like himself. It is clear this sort of 'behaviour' infuriates Zaid. He says – like so many hash gangsters – that his drugs are doing no harm to anyone. I guess it's his way of dealing with the 'business' he is in.

Meanwhile the high-pitched screeching noise of a speed

drill reminds us that the rest of his gang are unscrewing the inside covers of the Citroën's tailgate. They then start loading small brick-shaped packs of clingfilm-wrapped hash into all available crevices of the Citroën.

Zaid explains that this shipment of hash is due to go cross-country up to Madrid where one of the city's busiest drug dealers has a Rolodex filled with customers ready and waiting for the latest batch of high quality 'product'.

Zaid beckons us over to the back of the Citroën as his men continue packing the car with drugs in a meticulous and measured manner. Zaid picks up one of the clingfilm bricks and squeezes it gently then offers me the chance to do the same. It feels rock hard at first but then there is a certain amount of give in it when I try a second time. 'See? Just a few seconds of your body heat and it becomes softer,' explains Zaid.

He tells me this one brick of hash is worth €40,000 in Madrid. He declines to tell me exactly what he is selling it on for but I presume it was probably in the region of 50 per cent of that value. Zaid in turn would have bought it from his Moroccan connection for probably 50 per cent of that price.

I discreetly count the number of hash bricks being hidden into that little Citroën and there are at least fifty. That means this car is about to transport drugs worth well in excess of €1 million to Zaid . . . It seems incredible that such a small vehicle can be used to transport such a valuable shipment. But then again, it is clear that it is at this point the hash starts to make huge amounts of money for those prepared to finance its shipments. In a sense, the ones who take the real risks – the people in that Citroën – are nothing more than mules. Zaid says the two men in the car will get €3,000 each for driving the hash up to Madrid. Like any big business, it is the moneymen who stand to make the most profits. They are risking not themselves but their cash and that seems a more valuable commodity than human lives in the secret underworld of hash.

Zaid goes on to explain the costs and complications involved in getting the hash from the coastline of southern Spain to the cities of Europe. He is careful to point out that he has nothing to do with the Moroccan end of the operation, but he openly talks about who needs to be bribed to get the hash out of North Africa.

There are different methods of transport into Europe, but there is one main route from Tangier and the Rif Mountains beyond: across that already familiar stretch of water called the Strait of Gibraltar. The real players in this game deal in huge quantities and run sophisticated operations. Zaid even tells a chilling anecdote about how a gang of Dutch criminals tried to set up their own smuggling 'hub' in Ketama and ended up with their throats cut.

'These guys just didn't get it,' explains Zaid. 'They thought by cutting out the Moroccan transporters, they could cut their costs and make even bigger profits but they are the ones who got cut. It's madness to try and do business inside Morocco. Leave it to the locals, I say.'

Zaid openly admits that he himself comes from a family of Moroccans who immigrated to Spain three generations earlier. 'Look, even I who am part Moroccan know it is dangerous to step on their tails. Of course, I have used my family connections to set up a supply route. But I have been very careful not to put any Moroccans out of business during that process.'

But Zaid knows all the pitfalls when it comes to the hash business. He says he has dealt with everyone from the Brit gangsters – 'fair and strong' – to the Balkan underworld – 'evil and cold' – and he claims that a few years ago he found himself doing business with a shady bunch of Moroccans who turned out to be Al-Qaeda terrorists trying to raise cash to buy weapons.

Zaid explained: 'It was just before 9/11 so Al-Qaeda were more open about their activities and they had a cell of Moroccans working for them out of Tangier. The idea was that a bunch of Moroccan gangsters put up 50 per cent and Al-Qaeda the other 50 per cent and they shared the profits. But my friends the Moroccans said the Al-Qaeda boys were a nightmare to deal with. They didn't understand the complex nature of hash smuggling and expected their profits to come pouring in virtually before the first shipment reached Spain. Then one of them accused the Moroccan gangsters of ripping them off and it ended in one guy dying and two being badly injured. From that moment on, no one in Morocco would agree to do business with Al-Qaeda. Eventually they set up their own supply route from one 'friendly' hash farm on the other side of the Rif Mountains and transported the hash by road into Tunisia, where it was shipped across the Mediterranean to Italy.'

But Zaid says that after 9/11 Al-Qaeda's hash-producing farm was raided by one of the area's most powerful drug lords. After a two-day gunfight, Al-Qaeda retreated back across the border into Algeria, where it is believed they set up another hash farm. Zaid says that the way the local gangsters ran Al-Qaeda out of the Rif Mountains has become part of Ketama folklore. 'The Moroccans are very proud of getting rid of the terrorists,' explains Zaid. 'They feel they showed great loyalty to their country although what they really did was take the pressure off their own activities because the Americans are always pressurising the Moroccan government to close down the hash fields in the Rif Mountains.'

Back in that Algeciras warehouse, Zaid's men continue using their power tools to screw back the door linings of the little Citroën hatchback before it heads off up to Madrid. Zaid inspects the car after the operation is completed and claps two of his men on the back, congratulating them for a job well done. Now more relaxed, Zaid's voice softens as he talks about his career as a hash baron.

'I don't deal in coke or anything else like heroin or crack because I know the prison sentences are much higher if you're caught,' he explained before I even asked. However, Zaid claims that even the hash trade is suffering from the worldwide recession, which has hit especially hard in Spain. 'It's certainly true that up until about five years ago the profits on each shipment of hash were much greater. It's a strange situation because the demand, especially here in Spain, remains very high although people have less money so it will slow down eventually. But the costs involved in smuggling it from Morocco are increasing by the month. Today, we have to build in all sorts of expenses, which simply didn't exist a few years ago.'

Zaid was open about nearly all aspects of his criminal enterprise but was rather more reluctant when it came to discussing his family and how his 'career' affected them. 'I have a wife and two children. I'm a regular sort of guy in many ways. I pick my kids up from school some days. I take them to the beach. We go on vacations together. My wife knows that I am involved in a risky business. That is all she needs to know. It's important to remember that if I shared my knowledge with her then that would endanger her life because there are a lot of bad people in this game and they would stop at nothing to find out more about my operation.'

Zaid bear-hugs his two men before they drive off in the Citroën for the six-hour journey to Madrid with that shipment of €1 million worth of hash hidden in the vehicle. Before they leave the warehouse, Zaid and two other men check that it is clear in the street. Zaid then waves them off into the darkness for a trip that will personally earn him many tens of thousands of euros.

As Zaid is shutting the big double doors to the warehouse, he notices a vehicle parking up on the pavement about a hundred yards from the entrance to his building. He nods at his two associates and they lock up the doors while I watch them from inside the poky little office attached to the warehouse.

Outside, Zaid strolls casually towards the vehicle parked further up the street. It is only then, as I continue watching from the office, that I notice there are two men sitting in the car.

For the first time since I met Zaid earlier that evening, I feel a sense of danger and risk in the air. His two men who closed the doors remain silent and they urge me to keep quiet by putting forefingers to lips. So I am left with no option but to watch Zaid as he continues to walk towards the car with the two men in it.

The man on the passenger side rolls down his window and Zaid leans in. There is an exchange of words. Then I catch a brief glimpse of Zaid getting an envelope out of the inside pocket of his jacket and passing it to the man in the car. Zaid then strolls casually back towards us.

Three minutes later, he is back inside the warehouse.

'Relax,' says Zaid. 'Two tame cops who needed paying. They come round here every week and sit there until I give them some money. We look after them, they look after us.'

That night, Zaid and his men locked up the warehouse and insisted I accompany them to a lively local bar where beer and seafood was in plentiful supply. Zaid toasted me with a wry smile on his face. 'Good luck with your book,' he told me. 'Just make sure you tell the truth.'

For a few moments, it felt as if there was a threatening

tone in his voice but there again I might have been imagining it.

At the end of the evening, I tried to pay the bill for everyone but Zaid insisted it was down to him. Then I noticed the barman refusing any cash from Zaid . . . it seems that people like Zaid are not expected to pay for anything thanks to their reputation in the community.

A few months later, I got a call from my lawyer friend in Málaga to say that Zaid had been shot dead by a hitman outside his own warehouse.

What goes around comes around.

CHAPTER 5

KING OF THE COSTA DEL HASH

Spain became a very popular destination for British criminals on the run following the collapse of the extradition treaty between the two countries in 1978. When the thieves behind London's notorious 1983 £6 million Security Express robbery were spotted leading luxurious lives on the Costa del Sol it was even dubbed 'The Costa del Crime'. It wasn't until seven years later that Britain and Spain agreed a new extradition treaty when Spain joined the European Union.

In 2000, the then British Home Secretary, David Blunkett, finalised a new fast-track extradition treaty with the Spanish authorities, but it did little to stem the tide of crime rolling across Spain.

And still the Brits keep coming in. A seventy-five-year-old Briton was arrested by the Guardia Civil in 2011 on a yacht, crossing the Strait of Gibraltar, which was found to be carrying 1,038 kilos of hashish worth €1.6 million on the drugs market.

As it happens, my interest in the secret and lucrative world of hash had partly been fuelled by living in southern Spain between 2000 and 2007. Working on a number of books about real-life British criminals living in the sun, I'd found that for all their bravado about robbing banks and security vans in the 1970s and 1980s, the most successful ones virtually all made their biggest fortune from drugs.

Some had even paid the ultimate price and lost their lives in pursuit of that elusive drugs 'lottery win' which they believed would enable them to quit crime altogether and enjoy a long and happy retirement.

Take Great Train Robber Charlie Wilson: his underworld infamy came directly from that so-called Crime of the Century in 1963. But the £40,000 which each of the robbers ended up making from the raid was never going to be enough for these characters to give up crime. South Londoner Wilson was considered one of the masterminds of the GTR and even escaped from prison for more than two years in the middle of serving a thirty-year sentence for his role in the robbery.

But when he finally got out in the mid-1980s, he found the underworld had changed beyond all recognition. Blaggings and robberies had been replaced by drugs as the main source of income for top level London villains. Charlie Wilson, ever the pragmatist, soon acknowledged that he needed to get a piece of the action from drugs sooner rather than later.

So he moved down to southern Spain, the infamous Costa del Crime, and began financing and running some of the era's most lucrative drugs deals. At first he kept strictly to hash because he knew, like so many others, that the sentences were much lighter than for cocaine. But the lure of the 'white stuff' proved too much to resist in the end and he set up a second 'importation business' from his home near Marbella, which dealt exclusively in coke. Meanwhile his hash runs continued to operate but on a much smaller scale.

Wilson himself loathed hash as a recreational drug because of the way it seemed to dull your senses. Cocaine, on the other hand, improved one's reactions and kept one feeling on top of the world. He even told one criminal associate: 'Coke is the only drug that makes you a better operator. I love it!'

Eventually, Wilson 'transferred' his hash business to a young south-east London villain who went by the initials 'RP' to all who knew him. RP was a classic wild card, a man with a criminal pedigree as long as a blagger's arm and a reputation as a risk taker.

Not long afterwards, in 1990, ex-train robber Wilson was shot dead by a hitman in the back garden of his luxury hacienda near Marbella following a clash with another British gang in a row about a cocaine shipment. The London underworld presumed that RP would step into Charlie's shoes and take over his coke business.

But RP surprised many of his gangster associates on the Costa del Crime and in London by side-stepping Charlie's coke business and sticking to his drug of choice – hash. It was a clever move.

As one Costa Brit explained: 'All the coke boys were dropping like flies. They were either getting themselves topped like poor old Charlie or being banged up in prison, thanks to co-operation between the DEA and British and Spanish police, who were on a mission to rid the world of cocaine.'

But, I was told, RP was the consummate survivor. He was *the man* to interview when it came to the hash trade on the Costa del Crime.

My mission to find 'RP' in southern Spain began with a criminal enforcer (debt collector) called Tall Tommy whom I'd known for many years on the Costa del Crime. He knew RP very well. Tall Tommy said many in the underworld admired how this man had managed to not only survive but thrive by sticking to hash smuggling only and ignoring all the heavier drugs and people smuggling, which many of the gangsters in southern Spain now specialise in.

When I eventually made direct contact with RP through Tall Tommy, RP immediately put up a number of conditions before meeting me. The first one was to travel to a small port west of Marbella so RP could – in his words – 'see where the fuck you're comin' from'. I agreed, not really knowing what I was about to let myself in for.

So it was that a few hours later I found myself on RP's high-powered speedboat close to the Strait of Gibraltar. RP's £150,000 powerboat was kept in a sleepy little harbour well away from the flashy villains of Marbella and Puerto Banus.

RP described it as 'one of my few luxuries'. RP is proud of his wealth but insists he doesn't flaunt it openly on the Costa del Crime, where he is one of the few remaining Brits still 'active' in the criminal sense of the word.

RP told me he'd agreed to meet me only because of my own contacts in the London underworld, including one particular criminal who'd helped me with numerous book and TV projects during the previous twenty-five years and was 'owed a favour' by RP.

'This is the life I always dreamed of as a kid, and I'm not going to throw it away like most of the old gangsters who pop up round these parts,' shouts RP above the thudding noise of his twin outboard engines, while we chug gently out of the harbour entrance towards the choppy waters close to the resort of Estepona, a few miles up the coast from Marbella.

'Hash is like most businesses,' says RP. 'It takes a while to get up and runnin' but once you've cracked the right system you can make a fuckin' fortune. It took me a while to get the right people after Charlie got done but now it all works like clockwork.'

RP's fortune is earned mainly through vast shipments of Moroccan hash that travel the lucrative route between southern Spain and the UK and the rest of Europe – via the so-called 'drugs hub' of Holland.

'Holland is the key to my business. It's like a massive filter for all the drugs that come up from southern Europe. But the great thing about hash is that the police and customs just aren't that interested in it. Their priority is coke, heroin and ecstasy.'

Yet again, it seemed that hash had unintentionally been allowed to flourish as a recreational drug because law enforcement in the West concentrated more on the more notorious harder narcotics.

RP continues: 'A lot of villains thought I'd missed a trick when I refused to get dragged into the coke game after Charlie got killed. Coke meant big profits with small quantities but it also meant dealing with psychotic Colombians, not to mention the arsehole Brits who put a hit on Charlie. I'd rather deal with a few nutty, sneaky Moroccans any day. The Colombians really believe the cocaine industry belongs to them and no ever gets away with fuckin' them about. Far smarter for me to sidestep the whole coke game. It's a decision I have never regretted.'

But, admits RP, the risks when it comes to dealing in hash are just as deadly. 'Look, it's a simple equation. The smuggler who makes the most money is the one who takes the biggest risk, especially when shifting large quantities. I've got a reputation round these parts. Trouble is when you make a fortune, others start wondering if they can get a piece of it for themselves.'

That, says RP, is why he is always prepared to 'pull out the heavy brigade' if any criminal rivals threaten his 'business'.

RP breathlessly recalled an incident in 2010 when a bunch of 'killer Bulgarians' tried to muscle in on his hash trade by forcing his Moroccan supplier to switch allegiances to them.

'They put a shooter down my man's throat and he nearly shat himself. I had to show strength by going in mob handed to see the Bulgarians and telling them to get lost. Luckily they backed off. It could have been a bloodbath.'

That brings me to the sensitive subject of 'losses'. I ask RP what happens if one of his smuggling teams lose a shipment as had happened to one contact of mine whose yacht sank off the coast of Majorca and who ended up with a price on his head because his criminal bosses held him personally responsible for that shipment.

'Well,' says RP, hesitating for the first time since we met. 'That's a tricky one because the shipment is the sole responsibility of that crew. If they lose it they have to repay me. That's the rule of the game.'

'Yes,' I ask. 'But if it was an accident would you still chase the guys who lost the shipment?'

RP looks a little awkward before answering. ''Fraid so. It's the law of the jungle. That crew is responsible. I would have put up tens of thousands of pounds for that shipment in the first place. It's their job to look after the produce.'

I hesitated for a moment then asked the hardest question of all: 'Would you have a man killed if he lost your shipment and had no way of paying you back the money that it cost?'

RP took a deep breath and nodded very slowly.

'I'll pass on that question if you don't mind.'

As the powerboat noisily tossed and crashed through the Mediterranean waves, RP pointed towards the imposing Rock of Gibraltar, probably in an attempt to change the subject.

'There's more villainy going on there than anywhere else. It's a hotbed of crime,' says RP. The crowded stretch of waterway between the Rock and Spain is policed by the UK's Royal Navy and also the Gibraltar police, as well as the Spanish authorities. Caught smuggling in this stretch of water, and you'll end up doing time on the Rock or in a stinking cell in the notorious Alhaurín Prison, in nearby Málaga.

But then RP knows all about being locked up. Back in 1981 he got a five-year stretch for holding up a security van in a London suburb. Inside jail, RP – considered a rising young star back then – made friends with some of the old-time professional gangsters and through them made invaluable contacts for when he was released. It was those connections that led him to run ex-Great Train Robber Charlie Wilson's hash business for him in the late 1980s.

Even now, RP looks back on those days with a sense of genuine nostalgia. 'It was like a breath of fresh air when I arrived in Spain. I was used to the police crawling all over us in south London but here the cops could be softened up with a few quid and maybe a gram of coke or a lump of hash. No wonder the British villains thrived out here back then.'

In those early days after his arrival in Spain, RP travelled regularly to Morocco to keep close tabs on Charlie Wilson's North African hash 'partners'. Eventually Wilson signed the hash business over to RP to concentrate on the fat profits he was making from cocaine. RP's career should have then come to an end when he got a two-year sentence after being arrested during a raid by police on a hash warehouse just outside Tangier. 'But I managed to keep the hash business going while I was inside, so it was still there for me when I got out,' he explains.

That stretch in a prison in the Moroccan capital of Rabat also helped RP learn a smattering of Arabic, as well as fuelling his own taste for 'smoke'.

'I'd steered well clear of using hash until I ended up in that prison where I smoked what is still the best hash I have ever tried to this day,' adds RP. He also admitted something that most hash barons refuse to concede: 'Hash is not as harmless as all us villains try to make out. I got hooked inside jail and it took a lot of effort to get off it when I was released. It makes you lethargic and deadens your senses, which is something you don't want happening in this game.'

Just then, RP turns his boat sharply to the right and we crash through a couple of white horses with a bang. 'What a life, eh,' he says nonchalantly. 'Sun, sea and plenty of dosh. There's nothing like it anywhere else in the world.'

A few minutes later, the vessel surges closer to the Spanish mainland just east of Gibraltar. RP points in the direction of a stretch of beach near a housing estate. RP says it is a popular landing spot for hash smugglers, where the drugs are collected in rubber inflatable dinghies and brought back to the beach to be loaded into vehicles. The gangs work differently though: some land the drugs, pack them into cars and leave car keys in various bars and restaurants for the next smuggling chain to move the drugs on. Others rent a nearby house with a good-sized garage and store the hash for a few days before moving it on to its next purchaser.

'Deserted beaches in the middle of nowhere are no good because the police make a special point of keeping an eye on them,' explains RP. 'Much better to land the hash on beaches near houses. Makes more sense all round.'

With that RP swings his powerboat back along the coastline and heads further eastwards towards the sleepy little harbour where he keeps the vessel. It's so isolated that as we tie up the boat, the harbour is deserted.

An hour later, RP and two of his henchmen drive me to one of those very same 'landing strips' on the beach where many of RP's shipments have come into mainland Europe. We wander up the beach to a quiet *chiringuito* (beach bar) for a beer. RP's henchmen prove to be an interesting pair because they're father and son, although to look at them you'd think they were more like brothers. But we'll hear more about them later.

Halfway through the drink in the *chiringuito*, RP recalls how one of his Dutch 'partners' recently got himself killed after trying to muscle in on other criminals' hash territory in Scandinavia. 'I told him not to do it. But he was a typical Dutchman. Thought he knew best. They're arrogant bastards. This fella got it in his head that the Swedes and Norwegians were particularly big fans of hash and convinced himself it was an untapped market. Silly sod. He didn't realise the bloody Serbs had got there first.'

He went on: 'As soon as they heard from one of the Hell's

Angels gangs who sell hash over there that my mate was planning a big hash drop through Denmark, they came down on him like a ton of bricks. They waited until he left his flat in Amsterdam one night and a motorbike sped past with a shooter on the pillion seat. Bang. Bang. He was gone. Stick to what and whom you know best. That's what I always say.'

Just then RP took a mobile call outside the bar away from my earshot. He walked back in stern-faced and announced that he had to go and 'sort out a problem'.

As he shook my hand before getting into his brand new Range Rover, RP stopped for a few last words: 'It's a crap shoot out here. One day I'll either retire with a fortune and live the rest of my life in peace and harmony or I'll end up like poor old Charlie with a bullet in my head.'

Then he hesitated and turned to his two henchmen and said: 'You two have got quite a story to tell. Go and have a beer together and see what you can cook up.'

The two henchmen looked a bit bewildered at first. Then RP barked: 'Go on. He won't bite you.' Then he turned to me and said, 'These two know where all the bodies are buried.' Then he turned back towards them. 'Don't you, boys?' It turned out that RP was absolutely right.

CHAPTER 6

JEFF AND PAT –
KEEPING IT IN THE FAMILY

RP's two henchmen were not exactly keen on talking to me at first, so I told them all about myself and eventually they seemed satisfied and agreed to tell me their story.

Jeff C, 58, was no stranger to the inside of a prison cell. Having absconded from the British justice system he was then arrested in 1995 and served three years in Spain for smuggling hash. He smokes hash every day of his life and outwardly promotes it whenever he has half a chance.

His son Pat is an altogether more tense, introverted character. Pat says he sometimes shares a spliff with his father but on the whole he tries to keep away from hash, except when he's handling it for 'work purposes'.

Jeff has worked for RP for ten years and he speaks fluent Spanish and French, which is unusual for Brit gangsters on the Costa del Crime. Father and son have had their own feuds down the years but at the moment they are working in harmony, which clearly pleases Jeff. He says: 'I'm proud of Pat and the way he's kept his family separate from all this shit. I wish I'd managed it.'

Jeff has been married four times (his first wife was Pat's mum) and he is currently living with a Thai woman he met on the internet. 'Pat's seen all my fuck-ups and he's determined not to repeat history. I respect him for it. I've screwed up good and proper down the years and I'm pretty lucky to have this little number with RP. He's been good and loyal to me because I've covered his back on a few occasions.

'I even tipped him off one time when some psycho Spanish villain threatened to go round to his place with a piece and a stupid plan to shoot RP. We calmed this fellow down eventually and everyone got home in one piece but it was a close shave for RP and he's always going on about how he owes me for that.'

Jeff's son Pat has a completely different take on the hash underworld. 'I've seen hash screw my old man up and he's bloody lucky even to have this job, considering all the shit he's caused in the past. I'm determined not to go down the same path. I've been very careful to keep my family completely separate from all this. I want my kids to grow up as normal, responsible people and have proper jobs and start families of their own in the real world, not this madhouse.'

Pat is built like the proverbial brick shithouse yet he talks with a gentle, almost feminine voice and seems to be constantly trying to hide his sensitive side from his outgoing father. 'I just want to get my work done peacefully and without incident,' he explains. 'It's not easy doing all this ducking and diving. You have to watch yer back every minute of the day and night. You never know who is on yer tail. It could be a rival firm or the cops. The main thing is to keep an eye open at all times and be one step ahead of your enemies.'

Jeff is far more cavalier about the risks they take, nearly all in the name of hash. 'This is the easier end of the drugs business. More often than not the Guardia Civil officers we come across are very sympathetic to hash smoking and tend to look the other way, as long as we grease their palms. I worked in the coke business in the 1990s and it was fierce. There was probably a killing every week of someone involved in coke out here in Spain. The money was huge but a lot of gangs would shoot someone just to make sure that others realised they meant business. It's no big surprise that a lot of them ended up being rounded up by the long arm of the law. This part of Spain needed to calm down and it's meant that the hash business has thrived.'

Jeff and Pat are responsible for organising all the beach drop-offs of hash for RP. He provides the cash they use to rent short-term houses near the beach with garages, so that the hash can be stored for a couple of days while it is broken down for distribution.

Pat admits there have been a few close shaves along the way: 'One time we organised a beach landing and were waiting for the boat to turn up with the hash when two

Guardia Civil officers started sweeping the beach near us with their spotlights. We tried to phone the guys on the vessel to tell them not to land but there was no mobile service! We knew it was only a matter of minutes before the police spotted us, so I took a huge gamble and walked right up to them on the beach and engaged them in a conversation.

'They were totally thrown and didn't even get around to asking why we were on the beach in the early hours. Then I took an even bigger gamble and offered them 2,000 euros to walk away on the spot because I had some hash coming in from Morocco. They looked at each other, smiled and accepted the cash and drove off. I remain convinced to this day that they only did that because it was hash. If it had been coke, they would have felt obliged to nick us on the spot.'

Jeff the father lives in a three-bedroom villa on a half-deserted modern housing estate between the seaside resorts of Estepona and San Pedro. It's an eerie place that has been abandoned by most of the residents. 'There are thirty houses here and only three of them are occupied,' explains Jeff. 'The rest of them were either never sold or the owners gave them back to the bank because they couldn't afford the mortgage repayments. Spain is in the shit.'

Relaxing in the sunshine at Jeff's home, next to his pool, Jeff reminisces about the good old days when he used to transport huge amounts of hash all over Europe. Back then, Jeff made regular hash-smuggling trips to and from Morocco on superfast inflatables with massive outboard engines.

They'd meet a ship, load the consignment into the boat, then take it to a waiting yacht, which would then sail to the UK, usually via Holland.

Jeff explained: 'Back then it was easy to sail nonstop to the UK without being stopped by local customs boats but these days a single yacht out in these waters will be stopped an average of about five or six times on a similar trip because the authorities are way more aware of the movement of shipping these days and they can monitor your movements by radar.'

Pat rolls his eyes as he hears his father look back so fondly on those 'good old days'. He says it's just a job to him. Nothing more. Nothing less. 'I know my dad likes looking back at those days as if they were more fun but they were also a lot more dangerous. These days we work out everything carefully in advance to make sure we don't get nicked. There is no point in being casual about it because then you most probably will end up in prison or dead.'

Pat adds guardedly: 'What Dad never seems to accept about this business is the biggest risks come from within. By that I mean that it is double-dealing villains grassing us up to the police who are the biggest threat to our freedom. The coppers themselves are pretty useless unless they happen to luck out and stumble upon us on a beach or get a whisper about a gang renting one of the villas near the beaches here in order to bring a load onshore and then store it in a garage for a while.'

Both men rate RP as a 'superb operator' whom they trust

with their lives. Jeff explains: 'He's a fantastic boss who knows this business inside out. He would never expect us to take unnecessary risks and he plans every job meticulously. I've done this sort of work as a one-man operation and it's a nightmare to organise. I feel much more secure having RP running things than if I was doing it myself.'

Jeff believes that hash will outlast many other recreational drugs because it's not considered as harmful as coke and the other Class A's. He explains: 'The eastern European and Russian gangs are obsessed with running the coke trade out here and they are welcome to it. They've muscled in on our territory but what they don't seem to realise is that the authorities are obsessed with breaking the coke supply routes, so they'll be the first ones to get nicked. In a way the cops are doing us a favour because the foreign gangs are vicious. They're obsessed with killing anyone who crosses them and they specialise in hits that take out entire families because they want all the other villains in southern Spain to be terrified of them.'

Only recently, a gang of Serbian cocaine barons ordered a hit on an entire Irish family near Marbella. 'They sprayed a hairdressers' with bullets from two automatics,' explains Jeff. 'It was outrageous. They didn't care who got hit. They just wanted to increase the fear and terror so that no one else would dare cross them. That's the way these bastards think.'

'Yeah,' interjects Pat. 'But that didn't stop you doing some work for them did it?'

Suddenly a black cloud between father and son looms over the proceedings. It seems that our conversation has touched a raw nerve between the pair. Jeff hesitates and gives his son a cold, hard stare. I sit in silence, waiting for them to either expand on the remark or drop the subject altogether.

'Come on, Dad,' says Pat, defiantly. 'Tell him what happened when you got caught up with that bunch of nutter Serbians.'

Jeff shifts uncomfortably in his seat, takes a long puff on a joint he's just rolled and knocks back a big mouthful of San Miguel beer. 'He's right, of course. Couple of years back I did some freelance work for these Serbians I met in a club in Puerto Banus one night. They seemed all right at first and I needed the extra cash because I was in the middle of a divorce at the time.'

Just then I notice Pat manically rocking back and forth on his chair. He has clearly heard this all before and knows precisely what is coming and just listening to his father talking seems to be disturbing him.

Jeff continues: 'I was a complete mug really. I agreed to use my smuggling skills to bring in a couple of shipments of what they said was hash. They promised me big money and paid half upfront, so I had no reason not to believe them.'

'Dad, they were fuckin' Serbians!' points out Pat, refusing his father's offer of a toke on his joint.

'Well, anyway. I rented a house near a beach in Estepona with a big garage and got everything else prepared for the first shipment, which was due in by inflatable. This vessel had been scheduled to pick up the hash in the middle of the Strait of Gibraltar from a yacht and bring it directly to the beach.

73

'The pick-up went as smooth as butter. No problems. No cops anywhere to be seen. The three Serbs with me seemed all right kind of blokes and we got it safely into the garage attached to the rented house within thirty minutes of the drop-off. I was very proud in a sense because I felt that was a good job done.'

Once again Pat, whose face is getting redder with fury by the second, butts in: 'Get on with it. Tell him what was really in those boxes then.'

For the first time, I can see how smoking hash keeps Jeff 'chilled' because I have no doubt he would have been throttling his son by now if it hadn't been for the cannabis in his system.

'For Christ's sake, Pat. Stop needling me.'

Jeff takes another crackling suck on the joint and then continues: 'The next day we all assembled in the garage to open and then repack the boxes of hash into smaller containers for the trip up through Spain and France to Amsterdam. I was just about to jemmy open the first big box of hash when this giant of a Serbian puts his hand on my shoulder and says "No". At first, I didn't know what the fuck he was on about. But then he kept his hand on my shoulder and gave me a big squeeze that really hurt!'

Jeff continues: 'That's when I knew there was something in those boxes they didn't want me to see. I turned and looked up at this fucking giant and asked him outright what was in the boxes. Was it coke? He insisted it was not and I kind of believed him. But I had to know what was really in the boxes because I didn't want to do the second shipment if it was something other than hash as that would make us a sitting target.

'That's when I noticed one of the other Serbs in the corner of the garage ripping open another much smaller box from the same shipment they were calling hash. The giant Serb tried to get me to leave the garage because he sensed I was not happy but as we walked towards the side door, I saw that the other Serb was gingerly emptying hand grenades into another smaller container.

'I nearly shat my pants on the spot. I'd just helped smuggle in arms and God knows what else. I was furious but also fucking scared because I knew only too well that if the Serbs got wind of my disapproval they'd probably have me topped on the spot. So I kept calm and went into the kitchen of the rented house with the giant Serb, pulled out my own personal and rolled up a joint while I thought about what to do next.'

Jeff's experience in the underworld then kicked into gear. 'I decided not to say a word to the Serbs about what I had seen. Instead, I made out I was feeling really sick and went home. I called them later and said I'd been to the doctor and I had suspected cancer of the stomach. Even they didn't know how to react to that! I offered to help them with the second shipment of "hash" but they said there was no point in case I got ill again.

'I told them not to bother paying me up for the previous job as I felt bad about letting them down. Shit, I was lucky because they never came near me again and I avoided them like the bloody plague. I even deliberately stayed away from that club in Puerto Banus where I met them in the first place.'

Son Pat says he hopes his father learned a lesson from that close shave. 'I told my dad to stick to RP and his operation. No one else in this game can be trusted. In any case, who in their right mind would get involved with a bunch of psycho Serbs? Sometimes,' he said, looking across at his father, 'sometimes, Dad, you need your fuckin' head examining.'

To his credit, Jeff laughed at himself and admitted: 'You can say that again!'

The strange thing about this father-and-son team is that they are both their own worst enemies and they leave one with the distinct impression that one day they'll fall out big time with all guns blazing.

My next Brit hash man on the Costa del Sol could not have been more different . . .

CHAPTER 7

BARNY

Just a few streets away from where hundreds of thousands of UK and European tourists spend their summer holidays on the golden, sandy beaches of Spain's Costa del Sol is a network of desperate young people scraping a living out of crime. Meet Barny, the street hash dealer. His story provides a disturbing flipside to the untold riches and luxuries of the hash barons and gangsters.

Barny and a number of his childhood friends were left behind in southern Spain when their British parents fled the Costa del Sol after the recession struck Spain in 2006/2007. Property prices crashed and many people, including Barny's parents, abandoned their own over-mortgaged houses by the sea and headed back to the UK to live with relatives and friends. Barny – in his early 20s – was educated in a British-run public school located in the hills behind Marbella and his entire life has been spent in Spain, unlike his parents.

Ironically, that same school was attended by the children of many British gangsters, some of whom have made their fortunes out of the hash business. 'The criminals' kids always seemed to have cash and they looked down on pupils like me, who came from so-called straight backgrounds,' says Barny.

When Barny's parents dropped the bombshell that they were returning to the UK, it left him feeling completely disenfranchised. As he explains: 'There was no life for me in the UK. It's a country that means very little to me. This is my home where I have spent my entire life. I don't think my parents realised how difficult it would be for me to move. Most of my friends in a similar situation have also stayed behind, even though we are all struggling to survive.'

And that's where the nightmare for Barny and his friends really begins. There are few work opportunities in southern Spain. Even jobs as a waiter are hard to come by. Restaurants are closing at the rate of twenty a month in the Marbella area alone. And, as Barny explains, 'The ones that are still open tend to be owned and run by families, who only employ their own relatives and friends.'

So, in order to survive, Barny has been selling hash for the last 'few years'. He says: 'It's a lot better than some of the things my other friends are having to do. Two girls I went to school with turned to prostitution to survive. They work in the brothels that are semi-legal out here. They hate it but they have no choice.'

The streets around the once opulent resort of Marbella

and its glitzy neighbour Puerto Banus used to be crammed with expensive sports cars and designer-dressed men and women. Now there is an overwhelming feeling that the place has been deserted by the *richerati* and abandoned by many residents too poor to afford to live there any more.

'I don't think people back in the UK realise just how poor Spain has suddenly become. It's almost as if it is sliding back into being a third world country after thirty years of success,' says Barny.

Since the 1960s Spain's economy has relied heavily on tourism and the construction industry which, to a certain extent, went hand in hand. As Barny points out: 'The biggest problem out here is that everything is expensive to buy but no one has the money to pay for it. My parents relied on cheap remortgaging to stay afloat and it worked brilliantly as long as our house kept increasing in value. But once the crash came many properties, including ours, went into negative equity and everyone fell into the same big black hole.'

Barny was first introduced to hash by one of his teachers at school who offered him a drag of his joint on a school trip when Barny was just fourteen years old. 'I got hooked on it real quick. By the time I was fifteen I was smoking hash every day and stealing from my mum's purse to pay for it. I never realised back then how it slows you down and makes you lethargic and apathetic. I fell into all the classic traps associated with hash.

'My parents knew I was smoking it but because I stayed

in my room virtually all day long they did little to try and stop it. I think they found it easier to handle me on hash because at least I wasn't out causing trouble like some of my other friends.'

Then, shortly after he left school, aged eighteen, Barny's parents' money problems came crashing down on them – and that proved to be a big wake-up call for Barny. He explains: 'I'd turned into a complete pothead and, quite frankly, I'd hardly noticed what was happening with my dad's work. He was a property developer without any property to develop. But when he told me they were planning to return to the UK, I freaked out. I felt like they were abandoning me, although they wanted me to go with them. But I'd only been to the UK a few times in my entire life. Spain was my home.

'My parents took off back to the UK pretty quickly after trying and failing to persuade me to join them. It was awful saying goodbye to them but I just couldn't face a new country with new rules. But at least their decision to leave made me stop and think about my overuse of hash at the time and I actually gave it up and tried to start looking for a job.'

Despite hundreds of applications, Barny failed to even get one job interview on the Costa del Sol. 'I was willing to try anything but jobs were so thin on the ground out here and there was some prejudice against me because I had an English name. It meant I got dismissed by many possible employers before they even met me.'

After months of struggling in Spain, Barny came across an

older Brit called Al, who knew some of Barny's schoolfriends because he was their hash dealer. 'I got talking to Al and he said that despite the recession the demand for hash was as big as ever. We both reckoned it was probably because it's cheaper to smoke hash than drink alcohol, which kind of makes sense.

'Anyway, he said he needed a "runner" to make deliveries to some of the urbanisations [estates] on the west side of Marbella and that he would pay me a basic salary if I worked for him every day of the week. By this time, my parents had gone and I had been sleeping on a friend's floor. I jumped at the chance of any job, even an illegal one.

'With my salary from Al the hash dealer, I could do a flat-share with two other old school friends. It was like a weight lifting from my shoulders. Thanks to the job with Al I could look forward to a proper future in Spain.'

Also, Barny admits that after his parents left Marbella, he found life a lot less stressful. 'They'd been in such a meltdown after the recession started hitting hard that they were rowing all the time and the atmosphere at home had been crap. Quite frankly, I was glad to see the back of them.'

But then nine months after starting work as a 'runner' for Al, Barny's life turned upside down when he got the news from London that his mother had been killed in a car crash. 'I was completely numbed by what happened to Mum. I felt so detached by this time because they'd moved to the UK and yet I felt heartbroken all the same. I rushed back to London to console my dad but he was a broken man. He was also angry with me for not coming back with them in the first place. He was virtually blaming me for her death. Also I felt completely out of place with my relatives in London.'

Two weeks after his mother's funeral, Barny took the decision to head back to Spain. 'Sure I felt bad. It was as if I was abandoning my dad but nothing I said or did seemed to make him happy, so I convinced myself he'd be better off without me. It probably wasn't true but it gave me an excuse to head back to Marbella.'

But by the time Barny returned to Spain, he found that hash dealer Al had replaced him with a new 'runner', a pretty brunette girl whom Al believed could keep his customers much happier than Barny did. 'I guess I was pretty naive to think no one would try and nick my job with Al. The young people out here are all as desperate as me and this girl was very attractive so I could see why Al preferred her to me. But it was a terrible blow. I had no money to pay the rent on the flat-share. My mates were threatening to turf me out and it felt as if my life had gone backwards once again.'

That's when Barny says he 'reached rock bottom'. He explains: 'I moved out of the flat-share. Well, actually they kicked me out and threw all my stuff out of the balcony onto the pavement below. I had nowhere to turn, so I started sleeping rough on the beaches near where I used to live. I'd eat scraps of food I found in dustbins outside restaurants and supermarkets. I slept in little coves on beaches I knew from my childhood but I had to keep moving because

I was afraid of being arrested for vagrancy by the Policia National.'

Barny admits: 'I was wandering around in a daze of depression and hopelessness. I simply didn't know where to turn. I slept in doorways and beaches and even on benches but I was running out of options. I kept wondering if my dad was okay back home. I had no money so I found a phone box and called my dad *cobro revertido* [reverse charges]. When he heard it was me he refused to accept the call. I was so upset I started crying in the street. At that moment I felt like the loneliest person in the world. My family didn't want me. My friends had tossed me out of the flat we shared. It had got so bad that when I passed old school friends in the street they'd turn their heads away and ignore me.'

Later that same evening, Barny met another older man who was also 'on the road'. He explains: 'This guy was English, from up north and he seemed a decent sort. We ended up deciding to put our heads down on a quiet strip of beach I knew from my childhood. Then, suddenly in the middle of the night I woke up after hearing a lot of movement in the darkness.

'I didn't open my eyes at first because I wanted to stay asleep for as long as possible. Then suddenly I felt someone on top of me. It was the man trying to rape me. I pushed him away but he was strong and got me in an arm lock and tried to make me kneel on the sand. I said I wasn't gay but that seemed to make him even more angry. He ordered me to drop my trousers but I refused. Then he weakened his grip on my wrists for a split second and I lashed out at him and turned and kicked him incredibly hard in the balls. It was only then I realised he was completely naked.'

Barny continues: 'I took off and ran and ran for at least a mile to make sure he couldn't find me. I decided there and then I had to get my act together and get some money together. I thought about all the things I could do to earn a living and concluded that selling hash was probably the safest option. I knew where Al got his supplies from and I knew I had to be careful not to sell on his patch but it was my only option.'

Within a month Barny had a list of clients, thanks to his connections inside Marbella, and enough money to try and lead a 'normal' life.

Now, more than two years later, Barny says he's desperate to move away from the hash business and try to make something of his life. But with the recession in Spain worsening by the month, there seems little chance of that.

He continues: 'I've had a few near misses while working as a hash dealer but nothing particularly dangerous. Most of the people I deal to are good old-fashioned dopeheads, who wouldn't harm a fly. I even bumped into Al not long after I set up business and he wished me well, just so long as I didn't start flogging hashish in his area.'

The biggest problem, says Barny, is when the professional gangsters who supply the hash to him decide to suddenly up their charges or simply fob him off with substandard product. 'That's when it gets a bit dodgy. These guys are out and out criminals, unlike me. If I show weakness to them they try to bully me and exploit it. A couple of times I've had a gun pulled on me because I stood up to them. Funnily enough that is the best way to deal with them because then they at least show you a measure of respect.'

One of Barny's most regular suppliers of hash is a local policeman. 'This guy actually approached me through another customer,' he says. 'I thought he was pulling my leg at first then he explained that his police station confiscated literally tons of hash every year and it was supposed to be burned in an incinerator each month. But he said that it was never closely checked and it was easy to steal huge lumps without anyone noticing. I was obviously wary at first but this cop proved to be as good as gold when he turned up as promised at a pre-arranged rendezvous with a brick of the best hash I had ever come across!'

However, Barny remains convinced he is treading a dangerous path if he stays in the hash game for too long. 'I've noticed that the dealers who are clever never stay in this profession for too long. They say that once you start thinking about stopping you should quit immediately because if your head goes, then you start making mistakes and once you do that you're basically fucked and something bad will happen to you sooner or later.'

Barny mentions the case of another smalltime dealer working on the perimeter of Barny's 'territory' who ended up getting 'a very brutal lesson'. 'This guy bought a load of hash off an Albanian who I have always managed to avoid, thank God. Anyway my mate didn't have the full amount of cash required when he took a delivery of this guy's hash but then the stupid idiot forgot to pay up when he next saw the Albanian. A few days later a man with a gun knocked on my mate's door and when he answered he got the bullet – literally. He wasn't killed but he hasn't had a job of any kind ever since.'

But the most harrowing anecdote of all from Barny came when he told how another young dealer he knows lost a shipment of hash that he was handling for a major criminal. 'They tracked down this young dealer, smashed the front door down of his flat and when he said he couldn't pay for the lost shipment they hauled him off to a gay brothel in Estepona and forced him to work off his debt. In the end the guy did a runner and the last I heard of him he was somewhere in northern Spain working for a really nasty gang of Colombians.'

So how is Barny ever going to escape the clutches of the hash trade? He explains: 'I've saved up a lot of cash and when the moment is right I will make the move. I know it has to be sooner rather than later otherwise I could end up in the same shallow grave as a few of the other dealers round here.'

Barny's story is both sad and revealing. He has used hash to survive but, ultimately, he is more a victim than a criminal and he longs for a life of normality and happiness like everyone else.

CHAPTER 8

INSIDE SPAIN'S 'HASH CENTRAL'

Alhaurín de la Torre Penitentiary, near Málaga, on the Costa del Sol, is renowned as Spain's most overcrowded prison with more than 2,000 inmates. It's designed to house only 900 prisoners. It also happens to contain more hash offenders than probably any other jail in the world.

Attacks against prison guards and among the inmates are infrequent because the regime is relaxed in many ways. Many inmates have mobile phones and it's said that all the staff are bribable, if the price is right.

However, my visit to Alhaurín coincided with the discovery of the body of a twenty-one-year-old prisoner in his cell, who'd swallowed more than a dozen capsules of hash. His cellmate reported that the youth was ill and lying on the cell floor. He died a short while later.

The dead man had only been in Alhaurín for forty-eight hours but he'd swallowed the hash while being transferred from Puerto III prison in Cadiz in order to make a court appearance in nearby Melilla. Word on the prison corridors was that the man had been given the hash to swallow by a guard.

Alhaurín prison is certainly a foul-smelling hole of a place. The waft of sweat, fear and loathing hits you in the face the moment you walk through the gates, despite the pungent aroma of disinfectant. Everything is off-white in colour, from the faces of the deadpan guards to the chipped walls and the yellowing metalwork of the gated doorways. It's a strangely muted place, though, which is surprising because this imposing building houses some of the most dangerous drug gangsters in the world. And it's all just a few kilometres from Europe's number-one holiday destination.

Alhaurín itself sits on a flat plain beneath a vast mountain range, which is rumoured to contain numerous graves of dead drug smugglers and other criminals. It's what they call a modular prison, which means that there are five different blocks that house different classifications of prisoners; perhaps more surprisingly, there is even a women's block, although the men and women's sections of this prison are not directly connected for obvious reasons.

One British criminal who spent many months in Alhaurín told me that the inmates reckoned the authorities deliberately house the women just within sight so that 'we really suffer'. He said that it was possible to wave to the women in their cells and that sometimes inmates managed to form some kind of long-distance relationship but it all sounds very frustrating and simply adds to the dead, tinderbox atmosphere inside Alhaurín.

From a distance, the prison resembles a cluster of rundown, low-rise tower blocks, right slap-bang in the middle of a desolate rocky terrain looking down towards the sea and the mass of concrete that makes up the vastly overdeveloped Costa del Sol. When Alhaurín was first built, most of the coastal resorts were nothing more than fishing villages dotted along a picturesque, deserted coastline. Now the Costa del Sol looks like a sprawling mini-Rio de Janeiro dominated by bland tower blocks and depressing-looking estates of private holiday homes, jerry-built at high speed during the boom years of the 1990s. Many of them are empty and deserted since the Spanish recession started in 2007.

Inside Alhaurín, the grim-faced guards search all visitors in a casual, nonchalant manner, which belies the sort of security one would expect inside the biggest prison in the vast southern region of Andalucia. These 'screws' seem deadened by the sheer flatness of the atmosphere that pervades in this bland environment. They are poorly paid and it shows.

I was in Alhaurín to meet Billy, a notorious veteran British criminal based on the Costa del Sol. He'd been arrested a few weeks earlier while dropping off a shipment of hash at the home of another criminal who happened to be under police surveillance because he was suspected of being a major arms dealer, as well as a drug baron.

My visit inside Alhaurín was shrouded in secrecy because

the only way I could get in was to pretend to be a friend of Billy. I'd actually interviewed him for a TV programme years earlier and kept in contact with him. A few weeks earlier he'd phoned from an illicit jailhouse mobile phone to say he'd been caught up in a police sting and reckoned he'd be in the prison for some months before his lawyer could get the courts to grant him bail. The legal system in Spain works in strange ways. Often a foreign criminal will be arrested, thrown in jail and told he will only be released to await trial if he can provide a certain amount of bail money. As Billy explained: 'That can take months and months and it wears you down. In the end, you cough up the cash – usually fifteen to twenty grand, and you get released and then you fuck off out of there as quickly as possible.'

The Spanish authorities would never openly admit it, but there seems to be a deliberate policy at work here. If the criminal provides enough bail money he or she can then disappear, saving the system hundreds of thousands, maybe even millions of euros in legal expenses and the cost of keeping that criminal in prison. As Billy explained: 'It's a lot cheaper to let me go as long as I leave the country than to sit there for twenty years soaking up all their cash. It makes sense in a way, doesn't it?'

The ratio of guards inside Alhaurín to prisoners is 20 to 1, which seems quite good compared with some of the other prisons I have visited around the world. Incidents of attacks on warders are pretty uncommon, too. But it took the canny Billy to explain the significance of that. 'The guards are no different from us, really. Most of them were rejected as policemen. They're badly paid and quite resentful about it, so they often sympathise with us, which means most of them are open to a bit of bribery and corruption.'

Billy had access to a mobile phone whenever he liked and if that was ever confiscated, his cellmate Leon had three more hidden in their cell. Warders even brought in extra food for inmates if they were prepared to pay for it and there was a special annexed kitchen area near Billy's cell where cordon bleu prisoners enjoyed cooking their favourite meals every evening. TV sets were even allowed in the cells.

'It all helps keep things calm here,' Billy said. 'The guards are all right on the whole. No one seems to mind the backhanders from the inmates to them, although they're not so keen on openly allowing drugs to be brought in.' But Billy then added with a wry smile, 'Mind you, I've had the best quality hash I've ever smoked here in Alhaurín. No one would dare sell bad stuff because we're all in here together and we'd soon find out who cut it.'

Yet despite the supposedly relaxed atmosphere in Alhaurín, it's not always a pleasant place to be in, by any means. 'There are a lot of prisoners here who should be in mental institutions. The Spanish just don't seem to accept that people do have psychological problems and prison is no place for them,' Billy told me.

Before Billy turned up on the Costa del Sol twenty-five years ago, he was a London-based university-educated professional musician with great hopes of making it as a rock star. Then he got caught up in a £10,000 hash deal and decided to head to the Costa del Crime. 'The guy I bought the drugs from got arrested and I knew it was only a matter of time before the police came after me. I'd heard that Spain was easy to operate in so I booked a flight, packed a bag and turned up here. I've never been back to the UK since.'

Billy quickly settled into the drugs, sex and booze lifestyle that dominates life for so many expats in southern Spain. 'Dealing in big shipments of puff mainly was so easy out here back then. The cops were so badly paid they never even chased up cases,' explained Billy. 'They took the attitude that just as long as the criminals were only dealing in hash then they wouldn't bother with them. In any case, all the cops I've ever met out here all love hash and I always made sure that my favourite policemen got as much as they wanted.'

So for the following twenty years Billy built up a hash empire run through his own gang in the resort of San Pedro, just a few kilometres west of Marbella. 'Those were great days. I had a good crew working for me and I was making a fortune, spending it all on wine, women and song and even paid for my kids to go to private school. I had a top of the range Mercedes and a house bought for cash. I felt I was untouchable. And you know what? I was, in a sense. I dealt hash like a banker deals in stocks and shares. I was relaxed, confident and never had to get heavy with anyone. Most of the time, my team of lads did all the direct contact with the buyers, so I hardly ever had to get my hands dirty. It was a good system.'

Billy also made strong hash connections inside Morocco. 'It was really civilised. I'd pop over to Tangier every six weeks or so, organise another shipment, pay over the cash and then get my people to meet the boats when they came in.'

Billy reckoned that for fifteen years the hash trade in southern Spain was 'safer than working as an estate agent'. He explained: 'I looked on myself as a professional businessman. My wife and kids thought that was what I was. The money was rolling in. There was never any violence and I was on top of the world. I felt almost invincible.'

But then Billy got, by his own admission, 'too big for my own fuckin' boots'.

He told me his story. 'I bought this club which was basically a brothel and reckoned it would make a nice little sideline and I'd be able to launder all my hash money through it.'

'Clubs' as they are known in Spain are bars with bedrooms attached, which get around the anti-prostitution laws because the girls who work in the clubs 'rent' the rooms. 'The profit was in the drinks more than the sex,' explained Billy. 'You could charge ten times the normal amount for a beer and the girl had to pay you 25 per cent of her "fee" on top of that.'

But soon after purchasing the club and recruiting girls from as far afield as South America and eastern Europe, Billy was given a stark reminder of what being a criminal on the Costa del Sol had become. 'These two Russians walked into the club and pulled me aside and said they wanted a share of it. I was stunned and told them to fuck off. I couldn't believe they would have the bare-faced cheek to think they could lean on me.'

But that incident sparked off a vicious turf war. 'The Russians proved to be complete nutters. They kidnapped my Bulgarian girlfriend and told me they'd slice her ear off if I didn't let them take over control of the club. I was outraged. No one had ever tried to do this to me in all my years in Spain but times were changing.'

In the end, Billy paid a €100,000 ransom to the Russians and then hired three Romanian gangsters to 'teach them a fuckin' lesson'. He went on: 'That whole thing cost me close to a quarter of a million euros. One of the Russians was shot dead and I had to start hiring security staff to protect me and look after the club at all times of the day and night. It was fuckin' dreadful. I had to start arming myself around the clock and I ended up getting visits from three different gangs trying to get a piece of my club and drugs business off me.'

Billy says that today the foreign gangs are trying to run every single aspect of the criminal scene in southern Spain. 'They try to control the girls, the drugs, the people smuggling, the counterfeiting. I knew it was getting dodgy but I couldn't just close my operation down and retire to the Balearic Islands because I had mouths to feed and a business to run.'

Today, Billy recognises that he should have got out of the hash game then. Instead he ended up being arrested by the Spanish police when he delivered a shipment of hash to that arms dealer. 'No one would have taken any notice of that gun dealer in the old days,' he said. 'But the police terrorism unit was on his tail because they reckoned he was supplying terrorists with arms. I walked straight into a trap.'

Billy says he deeply regrets not shutting down his operation earlier. 'I knew all this was coming but like so many others I thought I was untouchable. I really believed that all these foreigners would shoot each other down and then it would just go back to the way it was all those years earlier.'

But Billy admits: 'Being arrested was a blessing in disguise in a sense because I'm sure I would've been gunned down by one of those psycho foreigners in the end.'

Billy predicts it's going to get even more deadly on the Costa del Sol. 'I've heard of people being shot over a 500-euro debt. It's got out of control and I can only see it getting worse.'

A few weeks after our interview, Billy slipped out of Spain following his release on bail from Alhaurín. Shortly afterwards, he called me to say he wouldn't ever be back on the Costa del Sol. He was heading for South America. 'That place is finished. It's on the scrapheap and it's about to implode. I reckon it's going to get even more deadly out there. I'm going to scrape a living together somehow but drugs are now a thing of the past for me. I lost my club, my house, everything after I was arrested and now I have a chance to make a clean start a long way from all the madness.'

CHAPTER 9

EDDIE, A MEMBER OF THE FOREIGN 'PACK'

It's not just the Brits who have turned Spain into the criminal badlands of western Europe. Today it is estimated that the Spanish coastline is home to more than 20,000 foreign gangsters of some seventy nationalities, including the Russian Mafia and armed gangs from Albania, Kosovo and the former Soviet republics. In addition to drugs there is a flourishing trade in illegally imported tobacco and cigarettes, which are almost as profitable to foreign criminals in Spain as drugs but with minimal risks.

Younger, flashier, mainly eastern European gangsters have been gradually eroding the power of the traditional Spanish and British hash gangsters out on the Costa. Many of these characters are based full-time in Spain. They stay mainly in the background as fixers and organisers, often hiding behind legitimate businesses while arranging big hash consignments, as well as committing all sorts of other crimes.

Drug investigations take up 70 per cent of police work on Spain's coastal regions. And according to Spanish officers, the typical hash baron these days is in his late twenties or thirties and often foreign. They are the sort of characters who'll walk into a bar or club and shoot someone to send out a message to rivals. *Don't fuck with me.*

These Spanish-based hash gangs use Uzis and even hire hitmen to send out a chilling message to anyone who dares to cross them. They often number fifteen to twenty hardcore members, some of whom may have grown up together. Violence can flare up when there is a 'crossover' such as a turf war or when a drugs consignment goes missing. These criminals often begin by investing in the burgeoning club scene and supplying synthetic drugs from Europe, especially Holland.

The vast number of drug busts in Spain underlines the role being played by foreign criminals. In recent years, gang bosses have cultivated their contacts in Spain and set up members of their own gangs to act as international go-betweens with hash smugglers. Those links with Spain have become even more sophisticated and their network of suppliers and distributors is often now second to none.

Many Irish drug gangsters fled their home country and headed for Spain after the authorities introduced the Proceeds of Crime legislation and set up the Criminal Assets Bureau following the shocking cold-blooded murder of

Dublin journalist Veronica Guerin in the mid-1990s. One infamous suspect is rumoured to be operating in southern Spain as one of the biggest suppliers of hash in Europe to this day.

His emergence has come since the arrest in Spain of an even more powerful gangster who was born in Birmingham to Irish parents. After that arrest, the notorious villain became the Mr Big in Irish drug circles on the European mainland and he has spent the past three years moving between the Netherlands, Belgium and Spain.

Spanish police allege that sadistic Serbian hash gangsters operating in Spain's capital, Madrid, gave a gruesome indication of the kind of brutality they were capable of when Sretko Kalinic, nicknamed The Butcher, along with others, tortured and killed a fellow gang member then turned him into a stew. After beating Milan Jurisic to death with a hammer, they skinned and boned him with a sharp knife before forcing his corpse through a meat grinder. Police say the gang made a macabre facemask from his skin, cooked his flesh and ate him for lunch. They disposed of his bones by tossing them into Madrid's River Manzanares.

Kalinic confessed to the crime after being arrested in the Croatian capital Zagreb in 2011. It is believed that Jurisic, who was on the run after being convicted in his absence of assassinating Serbian prime minister Zoran Djindjic in 2003, incurred the wrath of his gang by stealing money from them. Another gang member, Luka Bojovic, who was also suspected to be involved in Djindjic's murder (an accusation which he denies), was later arrested in Valencia, where inside Bojovic's apartment police claim they discovered documentation that supported Kalinic's spine-chilling confession.

Spain's current recession has meant that more than two million workers lost their jobs in the four years up to 2012, bringing the jobless total above the 4 million mark. This leaves Spain with one of the highest unemployment rates in the EU at 21.9 per cent. Many of those unemployed end up working illegally in the drugs trade, often for rich foreign gangsters like Eddie, who knows all the tricks of the trade.

I meet him in a darkened warehouse, in La Linea, southern Spain. Just a couple of kilometres across the bay lies the Rock of Gibraltar. Eddie is protected by heavily armed gang members and his identity is hidden by a vast hooded anorak and sunglasses, which makes him look a bit like a character out of *South Park*. Eddie explains the ins and outs of the hash business and how the global recession has affected business. We get an insight into the complexities of buying, distributing and selling large quantities of hashish and where the future of the business is heading on the Spanish mainland.

'Like every business in Spain today, the costs have risen and the value of the produce – hash – has gone down,' says Eddie, calmly. His accent has a hint of German and I later discover that he is Swiss born.

Eddie admits his grandfather was one of the first ever importers of cocaine into Europe from Colombia in the late

1950s. His says his father died when he fell from a yacht and drowned during a storm in the Bay of Biscay while smuggling a shipment of drugs from southern Spain to the UK.

Hash may be seen by many as harmless, but in Eddie's twisted world it's a ruthless business that has to be 'protected' with extreme acts of violence. He also pays the local police huge fees to ensure his business remains untouched. As he talks, Eddie's 'team' clinically stow more than half a million euros' worth of vacuum-packed hash into the underneath of a Mercedes van.

Eddie keeps thousands of euros in cash in a safe in his office so that he can dip into the money to pay bribes to Spanish police and local officials. He calls it 'tax' with a smile and he always factors in at least €10,000 in cash bribes for the really big hash shipments.

Eddie goes into his office, takes a bundle of notes out of his safe and counts out €1,000 in cash, puts it in his inside jacket pocket and explains: 'I always have this money in case of problems. Then I can pay off a cop or a politician immediately. That way I own them.'

Eddie cracks open a bottle of vodka and starts speaking about his career in the secret world of hash. 'It's been a roller coaster ride, that's for sure,' he says with a smile. 'But this is my life. This is my career and it will probably not change until the day I die.'

Eddie's gang are mainly made up of Spanish guys he has worked with for years. 'I may be a foreigner but we all go back a long way. It means I can trust them with my life. You have to have trust in this game or else you will end up dead or in prison.'

Eddie says that hash consumption in southern Spain has increased ten-fold in the past ten years. 'The kids are bored and broke. Hash is cheaper than alcohol. Nearly every person under the age of thirty regularly smokes hash round here. It's a way of life and that means there is constant demand for my product.'

Eddie's 'territory' is a 150km section of Andalucia between La Linea and Seville. He explains: 'It works like clockwork and the risks are low because my hash comes over from Morocco and goes straight out on the streets in this part of Spain. I sell to local "managers" who run their own gangs of dealers.'

Eddie believes the key to his success and safety is that he sells off all his shipments of hash within thirty-six hours of it arriving on Spanish soil. 'I like to offload it very quickly. The less time it is in my possession, the better for me. I get it unloaded and then taken straight to my warehouse where it is distributed to various cities and towns round here immediately. That means there is only a very brief period of time when the police can catch me in possession of the hash. It all makes perfect sense.'

But it hasn't all been plain sailing for Eddie. Five years ago he was shot in the arm by a Moroccan, who tried to rip him off by supplying less hash than promised. Eddie explains: 'I was very angry that this guy ripped me off so I went to Tangier to see him. We had a row and he ended up shooting me in the arm. He was a lousy shot! It was no big deal and in the end he supplied the missing hash. I stopped working with him after that but at least I'd sent out a message that I was not to be fucked with. It was important because in this game your reputation is crucial and it stops people abusing your trust.'

Eddie showed me the scar from the bullet wound in his arm. 'I call it my calling card now because whenever I want to make a point with another criminal I show them the wound and they understand that I will not be intimidated.'

As we knock back vodka shots and talk in his warehouse, the Mercedes van, which has just been packed with hash bricks around its suspension and under the floor at the back of the vehicle, fires up and three of Eddie's gang head off to Cordoba to make a drop-off. 'I only deal with local people. It's much better that way. Whenever the British, Irish and eastern Europeans get involved it gets more complicated and risky. I stick to Spanish people. I trust them more.'

Eddie has only once fallen out with the local police – and that cost him a prison sentence when he was in his mid-twenties. 'I know most of the policemen round here now. They leave me alone much of the time. I give them cash regularly to show my gratitude. But a few years ago a new deputy chief from outside this area came in and tried to crack down on people like me. It was a nightmare because all my old police contacts had to step back into the shadows and pretend they didn't even know me.

'As a result, the cops raided a warehouse I owned at the

time and found fifty thousand euros' worth of hash, which was waiting to be taken up to Seville. They arrested me on the spot. I knew there was nothing I could do to wriggle out of it so I pleaded guilty and got an eighteen-month sentence, although I got out after a year, so it wasn't too bad.'

Like so many others involved in the hash trade in Spain, Eddie says that if he had been found in possession of that much cocaine he would have got a ten-year sentence. 'Even the judge shrugged his shoulders when he sentenced me. It was as if he was saying that there were more important crimes being committed out there and I shouldn't even have been arrested in the first place.'

Soon after Eddie was imprisoned the deputy police chief who caused him so many problems was transferred to another city. 'Thank God things went back to normal.'

With that Eddie lifted his glass of neat vodka and made a toast: 'To hash. Long may it continue . . .'

PART THREE

THE AMSTERDAM CONNECTION

I had so much cash flooding in, I didn't know what to do with it.

— Nils, Dutch hash baron

Holland has been the gateway to the European drugs trade for almost fifty years. But as far as hash is concerned, Dutch police are fighting an uphill struggle because the majority of citizens in the country are said to believe it should be legalised. Yet despite cannabis being tolerated in so-called 'hash cafes' in the main cities, the hash gangs continue to thrive.

In the middle of 2012, a special police unit found 15,000kg of hash valued at €47 million in the Rotterdam harbour area inside two shipping containers originating from Morocco. Police arrested four suspects. The hash was destined for the Dutch and Belgian markets. Police also raided several houses and seized €100,000, a firearm and ammunition.

Yet whenever Amsterdam and hash is mentioned in the same breath, most people think of those same dinky little cannabis cafes where student stoners sit round puffing on joints. But because of its pivotal location, Holland is frequented by some of the most ruthless drug barons on earth.

Take Henk Orlando Rommy. Born in Paramaribo, on the former Dutch colony of Suriname on 4 March 1951, Rommy's family eventually settled in Utrecht, The Netherlands' fourth largest city. By the late 1970s, Rommy was involved in used cars and stolen antiques. In 1977 he was arrested and convicted for trying to fence stolen art, including a Rembrandt, and sentenced to three and a half years in prison.

After his release from prison Rommy became heavily involved in trafficking hash to The Netherlands and Belgium. At one point he was arrested in Morocco and put on death row for eighteen months before being pardoned, allegedly because of the birthday of Moroccan King Hassan.

On Rommy's release, he went straight back into the most lucrative business he knew – hash. Working closely with notorious Dutch crime boss Johan Verhoek, he became one of Europe's most powerful drug dealers. When Rommy's Moroccan hash connection dried up in 1992, he quickly found a new contact in Pakistan, and began trafficking hash from there instead.

Rommy then focused on the Canadian and British markets and in 1993 Dutch justice estimated his organisation had an annual turnover of $120 million. Rommy had mansions throughout The Netherlands and Spain. But as his newly acquired nickname 'The Black Cobra' suggested, he was also a very deadly character.

On 4 April 2003, Rommy was arrested in Holland and charged with importing 1,000 kilos of hashish from Spain. He was found guilty and sentenced to just one year in prison. Thanks to a shortage of cells, Rommy was eventually released three months early.

Rommy's luck finally ran out when he was lured into a trap in Spain by America's Drug Enforcement Agency. He was extradited from there to the US. On 30 September 2006 Rommy was found guilty and sentenced to twenty years in prison where he remains to this day.

But even Rommy's activities pale into insignificance compared with the legendary Amsterdam-based Klaas Bruinsma. Reputed to have been the most powerful drug lord Europe has ever seen, he is known as 'De Lange' ('The Tall One') and also as 'De Dominee' ('The Reverend') because of his black clothing and his habit of lecturing others on the evils of drugs.

Bruinsma was born in Amsterdam and came from a middle-class background. While in high school, Bruinsma started using and selling hashish. When he was sixteen years old, he was arrested for the first time but then let go with just a warning.

Later he was expelled from school, and in 1974 he began working in drug trafficking full-time. Two years later, Bruinsma was arrested and convicted for smuggling hash. After his release from jail, he changed his identity to Frans van Arkel, aka 'Lange Frans' ('Tall Frans').

In late 1979, Bruinsma was convicted again for organising a huge hashish shipment from Pakistan. After his release from jail, he expanded his hash corporation further into Europe, to include Germany, Belgium, France and Scandinavia. In 1983, he became involved in a gunfight over stolen supplies of hash and shot several people as well as being also wounded himself. The following year, he was sentenced to three years in jail for this incident.

But none of this seemed to hit Bruinsma's highly profitable hash business. By the end of the 1980s, Bruinsma's organisation was said to be making millions of guilders per day. He decided it was probably time to retire but he was tempted into pulling off one last big deal by importing 45 tons of hashish. However, as soon as it arrived in the Netherlands, it was confiscated by the police following a tip-off from an anonymous source. Bruinsma was spitting blood and out for revenge because he knew it must have been one of his own gang who informed on him.

In 1990, Bruinsma and his British associate, a criminal called Roy Adkins, had a fight in a brothel over that same hash seizure. Shots were fired but nobody was injured. But Adkins was assassinated later that year and all fingers pointed at Bruinsma.

On the night of 27 June 1991, Bruinsma became involved in a verbal argument with Martin Hoogland, an ex-police officer employed by the Dutch Mafia at that time. Hoogland then shot Bruinsma dead in front of the Amsterdam Hilton at in the early hours of that morning. Hoogland was himself murdered in 2004.

These are just some of many cases, which prove beyond doubt that Holland's role in the secret world of hash remains crucial. Not only is Holland the drugs hub for the rest of western Europe, but its hash underworld has remained largely untouched over the past ten years.

CHAPTER 10

NILS

It's reckoned that today there are more hash millionaires in Amsterdam than any other city in the world. In order to get a real insight into the local hash scene, I tracked down a Dutch master cannabis baron I first met more than twenty years earlier when we both appeared on an Amsterdam TV programme about crime.

Back then 'Nils' was a flamboyant club owner. A sort of Peter Stringfellow of Amsterdam, who was more than happy to flash his wealth and influence around the city. He spoke perfect English like most of the Dutch and pressed his business card into my hand saying I should look him up the next time I was in Amsterdam and he'd show me a side of the city I would never be shown by anyone else.

I thought little of it until about ten years later when I noticed a story in the newspapers about Nils and how he'd been jailed for five years after masterminding what Dutch authorities were calling 'one of the biggest hash shipments ever seen'. Nils, the court heard, was laundering tens of millions of euros he earned every year from hash through three nightclubs he owned in Amsterdam, as well as a myriad of local businesses, ranging from a DIY store to, ironically, three legal hash cafes he owned in the city.

So I tracked Nils down through Facebook and sent him a message requesting an interview for this book. He replied within hours and I soon realised he'd lost none of his panache. 'Come and see me and I'll tell you the real story of hash in this city,' he promised.

My trip to see Nils in Amsterdam was to open up another side to the secret world of hash, which I had never even thought existed. For, since getting out of prison, Nils had, in public at least, turned over a new leaf and, in his words, 'gone legit'. I had no idea if he was telling me the truth but I knew that if I could get inside his head then I might get some interesting answers.

Nils's driver Harold met me at Schiphol Airport in a black Mercedes. He didn't say much on the journey into Amsterdam, except that Nils (at his own insistence) had reserved me a room in a very nice boutique hotel, which I later learned he owned. Just then Harold's mobile rang. He spoke briefly in Dutch to the caller then handed me the phone without a word.

'Welcome to Amsterdam,' said the unmistakably throaty voice of Nils. He instructed me to check into the hotel, dump my bags and then Harold would drive me to his office. It sounded like a sensible plan.

An hour later, I walked aboard the most luxurious canal boat I had ever seen. It looked modest from the outside and was tucked down a narrow waterway just off one of Amsterdam's busiest tourist areas. Now in his early seventies, Nils still looked the part, dripping in gold bracelets and dressed like a mobster from *Scarface* in a light brown double-breasted suit.

Unlike most criminals, Nils made small talk with ease and even sounded vaguely interested to hear about the progress of my book career since we'd met all those years earlier. I was embarrassed because I could barely remember what we had spoken about when we first met, so I let him do all the talking at first.

'You're a lucky man,' said Nils. 'Twenty years ago I would not have agreed to talk to anyone about the hash business. I kept it away from the surface because I knew the police were looking closely at my activities.'

Nils admitted he'd been 'a major hash trader' in Holland until his latest incarceration. 'No one could touch me back then, or so I thought. I had the main Moroccan routes sewn up. At one stage I reckon I had control of 60 per cent of the hash coming out of North Africa. I owned the supply routes and the Moroccan gangsters had to pay me for my transporting expertise.'

'What does that mean?' I ask.

'It means that I ran the port of Rotterdam when it came

to guaranteeing that the shipments got through. I organised the bribes and the officials would only deal with me. It gave them a sense of security because they were all afraid of being caught at the ports. I became the buffer between the crooked officials and the criminals. It was much more profitable than organising teams of smugglers and then having to find the dealers to sell my produce.'

I was beginning to realise that Nils had a unique role as far as hash smugglers and gangsters were concerned. 'It's a bit like being a movie producer,' explained Nils, lighting up a big fat Cuban cigar. 'I am not interested in just one movie. I want to produce dozens at the same time and that's what I did with hash. I was getting a chunk of virtually every hash shipment in and out of Holland. At one time before my arrest I was earning in excess of €250,000 every week.

'I had so much cash flooding in, I didn't know what to do with it. Yet I never once went near the hash itself. It was a beautiful deal. The risk was minimal and rewards were fantastic. I laundered a lot of the cash through buying property in Holland and Spain. I ran my three nightclubs in Amsterdam at a loss. I even invested in crap businesses just to be able to lose some of the money to stop the taxman and the cops looking too closely at me.'

Nils paused for a moment and opened a drawer in the desk in front of where he was sitting. He pulled out a newspaper cutting and smoothed it out in front of me. 'See? I even paid for an orphanage to be built. They wanted to name it after me but I knew that could bounce back so I refused and donated all the money secretly. This newspaper article talks about a secret donor but no one but the school itself knew I had provided the funds.'

Then Nils admitted that he had been an orphan himself. 'I know what it's like for those kids without families because I was one. If I'd had a proper childhood, maybe I wouldn't have committed any crimes, eh?'

As often happened with Nils, he was drifting off track. So I gently nudged him back in the direction of hash.

'Why hash? Well when I was about eighteen, I met a woman whose husband dealt in hash here in Amsterdam. It was the late fifties and cannabis wasn't well known back then. Most people looked on drugs as if they were the devil's candy. But I noticed this guy had a hard core of customers and they just kept coming back for more. The hash came from the Lebanon and Afghanistan back then but often nothing turned up and there wasn't any in the city for months.

'I could see that the people who used it wanted it all the time. It didn't make sense to have a product that was in demand which you couldn't get all the time. So I got this guy to introduce me to his supplier, an Arab based in Rotterdam. He told me he could sell hash every day of the week if he had enough of it.'

Within months, Nils recruited a dozen merchant seamen whom he promised to pay handsomely for bringing back hash from their journeys to Lebanon and Afghanistan. 'To tell the truth, I didn't care where the hash came from as long as I could get my hands on enough of the stuff.'

But, said Nils, it wasn't as easy as he thought it would be. 'Dealing with those seamen and the street dealers was a pain in the arse. I started bringing in shipments hidden under fruit and stuff like that. But some of that would go missing. Port officials here kept demanding bigger and bigger bribes. I started to wonder if it was all worth so much trouble. That's when I realised it was better to step back and let others do the dirty work.'

From that moment on, in the early 1970s, Nils turned his hash connections into a specialised Dutch-based criminal network that worked behind the scenes to ensure that the hash came safely through Rotterdam. 'Basically, I could guarantee any gangsters that their shipment of hash would get through customs here and then could be distributed to the rest of Europe. Without my influence, the hash would not get through Holland safely. At first, a few idiots tried to do it without me but they all failed and in the end they all had to come to me for my help.'

Nils claims that for the following thirty years he remained safely in the background pulling all the strings for hash shipments coming in and out of Holland.

But even a so-called perfect criminal enterprise can come up against a few problems. Nils explained: 'You get a lot of bigshots in this business. They are guys who think they're tough and they try to cut out the middlemen like me. They are bullies. I've had a couple of them come round here and pull guns on me but my answer to them is always the same. No one else can control the officials at the port and other points of entry. You can't just set up this type of operation overnight. It takes years of making contacts.

'I told one idiot to go and try and do it on his own and if he succeeded I'd hand over my business to him. Well, you can guess what happened, can't you? He got arrested and put in prison within months because he started openly offering bribes to people at the port. They told the police immediately and they came looking for him.'

But, I ask, how did Nils himself end up getting caught?

'Oh, that was just bad luck on my part. I had a fallout with a criminal who claimed that my men had stolen his shipment of hash as it came through Rotterdam. Stupid asshole had been robbed by his own men without even realising it. But this guy got obsessed that I was ripping him off and he started shouting his mouth off in Amsterdam. The cops got to hear about it and they put me under surveillance for months.

'I knew the police were watching me but I thought they didn't have anything on me. I didn't realise that this same bastard had been arrested and agreed to give evidence against me in exchange for a lighter sentence. In the end they filmed three criminals coming to my office for meetings and then combined it with the testimony from this guy and I got arrested. It was still a thin case but the cops were determined to make something stick.'

At first Nils continued running his hash empire from inside prison but then a corrupt officer he knew informed Nils that the police were building another, much bigger case against him. 'That's when I decided to quit while I was ahead of the game. I'm too old to go back to prison.'

Nils is still 'dabbling' in the hash game but he believes that as long as he remains low key, the police will not bother with him. It's hard to believe that someone as powerful as he once was would turn his back on such a lucrative trade.

So, how was he making the majority of his money these days?

'Hotels. Apartment blocks. Houses. I have plenty of property to keep me busy. I don't need the hash business any more and it doesn't need me.'

Who, then, had taken over his business?

Nils hesitated for a few moments before answering. Another couple of beats of silence followed before Nils sighed deeply.

'There is another, even more important reason why I quit. One of my best friends got shot dead in the reception area of one of my own hotels. It was a disgusting, cowardly act but certain people were trying to send a very nasty message to me and it worked. I realised I was too old to try for this game.

'I talked to my family and friends and decided to enjoy the rest of my life without these types of threats hanging over me. In the drugs business, the only survivors are the sensible ones who sit back and take stock of their lives and get out at the top. Acting rashly always ends in death and destruction. The smartest move I ever made was to walk away from it. I just hope it never catches up with me in the end.'

THE AMSTERDAM CONNECTION

That night I had dinner with Nils in the restaurant of his boutique hotel where I was staying. We never once talked about the hash trade again. He had said his piece. He'd allowed me into his world and there was nothing more to be gained by talking about it further. Instead, he spoke of his regret at never marrying and how if he had had better opportunities while growing up he might have made his fortune from legitimate means rather than crime. I had no doubt he meant every word he said.

PART FOUR

HASH IN THE UK

There are two million regular hash smokers in the UK. Unofficial estimates predict that that figure will double within the next 20 years.

Britain is, in the words of one law enforcement official, 'a very lively marketplace for hash'. That's understating it, to say the least. Britain has its own hash epidemic and with prices remaining high, it is attracting more and more opportunistic gangsters.

Back in the summer of 2007, a bunch of Essex villains tried to smuggle enough cannabis into Britain to make joints stretching from John O'Groats to Land's End. Two shipments of hash worth £11 million – hidden inside boxes of cucumbers – and weighing around four tons. The twelve-strong gang were foiled by the Serious Organised Crime Agency, who tracked the shipments from Spain to the UK in a covert sting operation. The hash gangsters were eventually jailed for a total of sixty-six years.

Around the same time, police in south London uncovered an Amsterdam-style hash smokers' den based in a popular Streatham restaurant, which pulled in hundreds of customers a week. Smokers could place their order at the counter before heading to a comfy basement lounge to light up. Officers later said they'd found portions of the drug packaged and ready for sale alongside tasty snacks and pastries.

That raid came days after three separate cannabis factories were dismantled across Newcastle in a twenty-four-hour period. In total more than 5,500 plants were seized, while data collected by the local newspaper suggested that residents are never more than a mile away from a cannabis farm in Newcastle.

But my intentions to uncover the British side of the secret underworld of hash for this book proved a hard nut to crack. Clandestine meetings in pubs, motorway service stations and isolated lay-bys occurred as I tried to unravel the UK end of the hash trade. Many of these initial contacts were middlemen who insisted on finding out more about my book project before putting me in touch with the real characters involved in hash. But the first batch of hash gangsters I encountered had little extra to offer following on from the British hash kings of southern Spain, so I bided my time.

Then one day I met a slippery character called Benny in Camden, north London, who said that he'd put me in touch with someone whom he guaranteed would give me a completely different perspective on the hash game. 'This bird'll blow your mind, mate. She knows it all inside out.'

So, that's how I came across Tina, probably the most unlikely member of the secret underworld of hash I was ever likely to meet.

CHAPTER 11

TINA

Tina is what they call a 'living legend' inside the secretive hash business. She's a light aircraft pilot from Suffolk, who's flown tens of millions of pounds' worth of Moroccan hash into the UK from northern Europe over the last twenty-five years. Being a woman in a predominantly male environment, says Tina, has given her a big advantage. 'Villains are typical blokes. They think they're hard and macho and tough, so when they meet a woman they just presume she's a bimbo.'

In Tina's case, nothing could be further from the truth.

Tina is a surprise package in many other ways, too. She went to a fee-paying public school; her father was the headmaster at the same school and her mother 'was just about the most prim and proper person you ever came across'. Tina had what she openly describes as a typical middle England upbringing. 'It was boring but safe and my parents expected me to go into something equally safe, such as working in a bank or becoming a solicitor.'

But Tina's grandfather was the biggest influence on her childhood: 'He was a pilot in the Second World War. What a character. I think I got my reckless streak from him. He wasn't scared of anything. He got shot down and taken prisoner in France and then escaped from a prisoner of war camp. I loved hearing his stories about the war. He seemed so much more interesting than the rest of my family.'

Much to the disappointment of her academic father, Tina hated school. 'I was a bit of a Tomboy. I just wasn't interested in all that girly stuff. I didn't even want to wear the stupid pleated skirts that were part of our uniform. I mucked around in class all the time but I was pretty good at sports, so they never actually kicked me out. But I must have been such an embarrassment to my poor old dad.'

From the age of fifteen, Tina claims she regularly drove cars illegally. 'I used to "borrow" my dad's old Rover whenever he was working at the school and drive it round the fields near our home. Then, as I got more confident, I started taking it out on the roads without my parents' permission. I loved the feeling of being in charge of that car and driving held no fear for me.'

By the time Tina left school at eighteen with poor 'A' level results she knew exactly what she wanted to do for a living. 'I was determined to be a pilot like my granddad. He'd died by then but I felt his spirit urging me on to do it. My parents were appalled and sneered at my plans but I didn't care.'

In further defiance of her mother and father, Tina initially got herself a job in a local supermarket and saved 'virtually every penny' to put towards flying lessons. 'My parents refused point blank to pay for flying lessons. They said they were a waste of time. But eventually my dad recognised just how determined I was and, to his credit, gave me some money for my birthday which, combined with my savings, gave me enough cash to book twenty flying lessons at a local airfield near our home in Ipswich.'

Within two years, Tina was fully qualified as a pilot and making a modest salary crop-spraying for local farmers, as well as offering a chauffeuring service for owners of small planes whenever they needed their aircraft to be picked up from other airfields. Another sideline was delivering people's new planes back from France, Holland and Belgium.

'It was a dream come true for me to be earning a living from flying but the money was pretty poor. I could hardly afford the rent for a bedsit and after an initial burst of excitement I didn't even find it very challenging.'

Then – in her mid-twenties – Tina agreed to travel to Holland to pick up a plane for a local Suffolk businessman. 'God, was I naive back in those days!' she exclaims. 'This guy paid me cash up front to fly the plane back to Suffolk. I thought nothing of it at first. I got the ferry over to Holland, stayed overnight in a hotel and then headed to the airfield first thing the next morning.'

She continues: 'The customs people at the airport were really suspicious of me at first but I presumed that was mainly because I was a female pilot. There weren't many back then. I had nothing to hide, so I told the customs officers I was flying the plane back to England. They checked my passport and flight plan and off I went.'

As she flew across the Channel, Tina got a radio message from the Suffolk businessman asking her to land the plane in a field a few miles inside Suffolk and pick him up because he was desperate to see his new plane. 'My papers clearly stated that I was flying into an airfield near Ipswich but since he assured me I would still eventually end up there, I agreed to pick him up.'

After what she described as 'a bit of a hairy landing' in the field, Tina's client was waiting by a car with three 'large looking gentlemen'. 'They were all very charming but I did start to wonder what was going on. The client took me to one side and said he had a "bonus" to pay me as his three associates walked straight to the plane.'

Tina noticed the other men unscrewing panels inside the plane. She asked what was going on and her client laughed and added another £100 to her fee. 'I still didn't quite get it.' Then she saw that they were removing brown bricks tightly wrapped in clingfilm. 'It was strange, because instead of being outraged, I accepted the "bonus" and ignored what the three men were doing. This man never mentioned what was in those packs but he made everything sound such a laugh that I kind of forgot to ask him.'

'Ten minutes later I took off with the client beside me and we headed for an official touchdown destination near Ipswich. Naturally the customs men were none the wiser.'

Tina later discovered that her client was one of the area's biggest drug barons. Within a few months, Tina had not only become his lover but she'd also decided that a career as a smuggler beckoned. 'It was all so simple and the money was out of this world. And if I am to be honest about it, I liked the feeling of knowing I was getting away with it. Funnily enough I've never taken drugs in my life but I guess the high I got every time I completed a smuggling flight was similar to what people experience from a line of coke or a good hit of hash.'

Tina and her drug baron lover continued their affair for five years, during which time she worked exclusively as pilot for his gang. But when they split up after a row over his refusal to leave his wife, Tina decided she'd be better off making her services available to the highest bidders. 'I was lucky in one sense because he wished me well when I told him my plans. I could so easily have decided to then tell the police all about him but I never even considered that.'

By this time, Tina's reputation as a trustworthy pilot was well known in the criminal badlands of south-east England. Her services were soon in very big demand. 'They all knew I'd been working for this man. I was reckoned to be a half-decent pilot as well as being someone who could be trusted.'

Tina admits she always worked on a 'no need to know basis'. 'I really didn't give a toss what was in the packages I was smuggling. As far as I was concerned, I was the pilot.

End of story. It was much easier that way. I guess I was also avoiding responsibility for the criminal enterprises I was involved in which, on reflection, was a complete cop-out. It was also madness to think I would get away with it for ever.'

But Tina had one golden rule when it came to the smuggling game. 'I always stuck to hash. My lover convinced me that with hash the risks were much lower and the prison sentences much more lenient.'

In late 2007, Tina flew over a shipment of hash with instructions to drop it on a cornfield just inside the Essex border with Suffolk. 'All I had to do was release a lever and two big boxes would drop onto the field.' But instead of approaching the field directly she swooped over the area as a safety precaution. That's when she spotted two white Land Rovers half hidden under a clump of trees in a small wood.

'Alarm bells went off instantly in my head.' Tina pulled the plane back up and swept up high over the vehicles before anyone even realised she was there to make a drop. 'I reckoned they had to be the police and radioed to the gang to say what had happened. There was no answer, which was even more worrying. Here I was running short of fuel with a load of drugs on board. What the hell was I going to do?'

Tina eventually landed at another isolated field about thirty miles away and quickly started unloading the boxes. 'They seemed much lighter than the hash I'd run in the past so I ripped one open and took a look inside it. It was cocaine. I'd have probably got a minimum of ten years in prison if the police caught me. I'd been paid just £3,000 for that flight. I was furious.'

Tina hid the boxes in a rundown barn next to the field. 'I rang the bastard who'd commissioned the job and said I wanted ten thousand pounds because of the risks and the earlier incident or I wouldn't tell him where the coke was hidden. He started threatening me but I knew he wouldn't do anything because he wanted that coke more than anything. He held his temper and I arranged a meet, took the money off him and then told him where to find his coke.'

Tina says that was a 'pivotal moment'. She explains: 'I decided to take control of my life. How fucking stupid had I been? All that time I'd thought that by not knowing what I was smuggling I would somehow be considered innocent. It was self-deluded bollocks and I'd finally realised it.

'I got in touch with all the villains I'd worked for and told them in no uncertain terms I would never do another drop for them ever again, unless I was guaranteed it was hash and not coke. They were all surprisingly understanding about it and said that there would be loads of work because most of them preferred dealing in hash in any case.'

Tina knows the dangers only too well, though. She talks about the murders, the close shaves and the network of gangs behind the smuggling rings and how she has survived them all – and emphasises again how she's never smoked hash in her life and has no intention of ever doing so.

'My biggest regret is that here I am, fifty-three years of age, and I'm single, unmarried and never going to have a family of my own. I've thrived on the excitement of what I do while forgetting there is a normal world out there.'

These days, Tina flies 'about half a dozen' hash runs each year between Europe and the UK for three different drug barons based in the south-east of England. 'It's not so hectic as it once was and I feel I've cut back on the risks by sticking to a handful of flights each year. To be honest about it, I don't feel the same "high" as I used to, just a sense of relief when I get back home in one piece after dropping off a load of hash in some field or other.'

Tina believes that her activities have long since been flagged up by authorities on both sides of the Atlantic. 'Since 9/11 pilots like me are looked at by the authorities regularly.' She claims that a few years ago she was visited by two officials from America's Drug Enforcement Agency (DEA).

'These two Yanks turned up at my house one afternoon and said they needed to know about some of the characters I had worked for over the previous couple of years. They didn't have any evidence against me but they were hoping I'd help them on the basis I was a weak link, a woman in a predominantly male world. That got me very pissed off and I refused point blank to confirm anything to them and it soon became clear they did not have any evidence to pin on me. They were on a fishing exercise.'

Tina remains convinced to this day that she was only cut loose by the DEA because of the US's obsession with prioritising terrorism. 'Once they realised I was not a terrorist they sort of pulled back, even though they are a drugs agency. That's where hash smuggling can help. If I had been importing coke or arms then they would have come down on me like a ton of bricks.'

Tina takes me to a deserted landing strip just inland from the Suffolk coastline. It's a one-hour drive from Ipswich and the area is deserted and sparsely populated. As the silver birch trees bordering the field rustle and bend in a strong breeze, Tina picks up a small branch and draws a map in the mud as she explains how the smugglers take it in turns to 'hire' this same landing strip from a local farmer.

She then takes me over to the far corner of the field beyond a clump of oak trees, laurel bushes and thick bramble. Just behind it is the twisted remains of a twin-engined Cessna crumpled up alongside a burned-out barn. 'We never did find out why this poor bastard crashed. I think one of the other gangs decided he was getting greedy and tampered with his landing gear,' explains Tina.

Just then a farmer on a tractor appears in the field next to where we are standing. 'Time to go,' says Tina. 'The farmers hate our guts but they're happy enough to take our money when it's on offer.'

CHAPTER 12

JANE THE MULE

Besides the barons, dealers and smugglers who've made fortunes from hash down the years, there is a small army of 'part-timers' – people who dip in and out of the secret underworld of hash and often pay the ultimate price for their involvement. These are the Mules – the characters who often risk their own health in a desperate bid to make a few thousand pounds, if they're lucky.

Wherever there is plentiful, cheap hash there are mules prepared to risk their lives and liberty to carry it. Every year dozens of people are either arrested or die after swallowing balls of hash tightly packed in plastic.

These so-called 'eggs' usually hold about five grams of hash apiece. And most mules are expected to swallow around fifty of them at a time. Many are forced into it by human traffickers and other criminals. Others are students hoping to make some extra money by reselling the product once they get home. There are even a handful of hardened drug smugglers who seem willing to take the risks.

In 2012, one such mule called Edward Myatt, 54, from Ballarat, in Victoria, Australia, was stopped as he arrived at Bali's Ngurah Rai Airport on a flight from India after he aroused the suspicions of customs officers. He was later found to have swallowed more than seventy plastic casings containing 1.1kg of hashish and four grams of methamphetamine, otherwise known as ice.

Myatt was told after his arrest that he faced the possibility of a death sentence under Indonesia's harsh narcotics laws. He was lucky. In the end he only got eight years and a 1.5 billion rupiah fine.

So when I met someone who knew a British woman who'd worked as a mule, I reckoned her experiences would offer a completely different angle on the secret underworld of hash.

The first time British nurse Jane worked as a mule was when she was a penniless eighteen-year-old student in Tangier without enough money to get home to Birmingham. She swallowed thirty pellets of hash in exchange for £1,000 and made it back to the UK to deliver the hash, despite one of the pellets bursting in her stomach.

Now in her mid-thirties, Jane has revived her career as a mule in a desperate bid to support her family. Since 2010, Jane has returned three times to her Moroccan lover in Tangier to swallow hash pellets. She says: 'I can't fully explain why I let myself be sucked back into all this but I guess it's down to a combination of things. My husband lost his job. My salary as a nurse simply doesn't cover the costs of bringing up my family and, if I am to be completely honest about it, I liked escaping the drudgery of my life and meeting my lover to do something exciting.'

Jane's story is both harrowing and fascinating as she unravels her involvement in the most dangerous side of the hash industry of all.

'I first went to Morocco as a student in the late nineties. It seemed a wonderful place and when my two girlfriends whom I was travelling with decided to go home, I opted to stay on my own in the city of Rabat. I'd fallen head over heels for this Moroccan waiter in the hotel where we'd stayed. It was a classic; he saw me as a great way to smuggle hash and I saw him as the love of my life.

'Anyway, about a month into the relationship, I told him I had to go back to England but I was broke. I needed to get a job and get started on the next stage of my life. He was furious with me for planning to abandon him and we had a massive row and I stormed off into the night.

'He came after me and we reconciled and he told me how easy it would be to earn a couple of thousand pounds smuggling hash as a mule so I could afford to get home and have some money to spare. I was appalled when he first told me. How on earth could anyone swallow all those pellets and then have the front to walk through customs at the airport? It sounded horrible. The idea of plucking those pellets out after going to the loo was even more disgusting.

'But my boyfriend promised me that if I did it, not only would I get paid but he'd also come out and join me back home in Birmingham and then we could set up home together and live happily ever after. What a load of old bollocks that turned out to be!

'When I look back on what happened, I cannot believe how gullible I was. It was as if all he had to do was look at me with those dark brown eyes of his and I'd melt. I even convinced myself that he was only doing this for us! So I agreed to swallow forty pellets and deliver them to a guy in a cafe near the Bullring in the centre of Birmingham a few hours after my flight touched down from Morocco.

'Just swallowing them was horrible in itself. I kept feeling like I wanted to vomit after putting each pellet in my mouth and swallowing. But with my lover standing there urging me on I continued. Then I picked up my bag and headed to the airport alone. He'd told me it was safer that way and I believed him. I never questioned anything he ever said.'

Jane recalls that the trip went off without incident. She got her £2,000 but her Moroccan lover changed his mind about coming over to Birmingham to set up home with her. 'I was heartbroken about his decision. It only dawned on me that he was using me when he asked me to come back to Morocco to do another mule run. I told him to get lost and that was the end of that.'

Jane says she then put her brief experience as a mule firmly behind her and took up a career in nursing, met and married a man she'd known at school and they had two children. 'For more than ten years I barely gave Morocco a second thought and I'd pushed those experiences firmly to the back of my mind. As far as I was concerned it was all in the past and I never once mentioned to my husband what had happened. He was a pretty straight bloke, so he'd have been horrified if he knew what I'd done.'

Then Jane went on a hen-night trip to Morocco with five of her best friends. 'I was like an over-excited kid about going back after all those years. It stirred up all these feelings about that guy in Morocco and all the exciting things that happened there in my teens. I even looked back on my experience as a mule as being such fun.'

A three-night stay in Casablanca with her friends proved even more raucous than any of them expected. 'Two of my girlfriends got off with young Moroccans on the first night and I got really jealous about it. I wanted one for myself. So on the second night I made sure I got picked up in a local nightclub by this gorgeous young Moroccan lad who looked about twenty. I was like an over-excited schoolgirl. Even my mates were a bit shocked when I started snogging this boy within about five minutes of meeting him.'

She continues: 'I completely pushed my husband and kids to the back of my mind and decided to really go for it that night. I ended up in bed with this lad and had the best night of sex since I'd been in Morocco as a teenager all those years earlier. Next morning, I started to seriously wonder if all this was fate. Maybe I should never have left Morocco in the first place? If I'd stayed with that first Moroccan lover we'd have a beautiful family by now and I'd probably have a damn sight better life than the one I had back in Birmingham.

'It was all a form of madness, I suppose. I was being swept up in exactly the same way I had been all those years earlier. My girlfriends kept trying to make me see sense but I literally couldn't see the wood for the trees. I thought I was in love again. I didn't want to go back to my sad life in Birmingham.'

What followed next was painfully predictable but it didn't stop Jane from falling into a duplicitous trap. 'I'd told this guy about my family back in the UK and how we were struggling financially and how my husband had lost his job. He seemed terribly empathetic for someone so young. Then he mentioned how he had a cousin who smuggled hash into Europe. My ears pricked up with excitement. All those memories of my earlier trip to Morocco came flooding back. I knew perfectly well what he was going to say before he even said it.'

On the morning of the hen party's departure back to Birmingham, Jane only just made it to the airport. 'I'd stayed the night with this lad and then it had taken me so long to swallow all the pellets that I only just got to the airport about ten minutes before the flight took off. But the funny thing was that I wasn't at all frightened. I'd done this before and there had been no problems, so I knew what to expect.'

'What to expect' involved swallowing fifty small hash eggs. Jane described it as being like swallowing sandpaper. 'At first you have to suppress your gag reflex. But I soon remembered how to do that and they all went down surprisingly easily.

'During that cab ride to the airport it didn't feel all that weird, though. Just like I had a very full tummy after a big meal. I had drunk a lot of water though, so I kept wanting to go to the loo, which was a bit of a pain.'

Settling down next to one of her girlfriends on the plane, Jane admits she then had a pang of guilt. 'They just thought I'd had a good shag and nearly missed the plane because of it. I felt bad because the girl who'd been getting married had paid for all our air fares, so if I got caught with the hash pellets she could be in trouble.'

But the flight went off without incident and Jane, in her own words, 'waltzed through customs in the UK as if I didn't have a care in the world'.

She then went to a hotel room, which had been pre-booked for her in the centre of Birmingham and waited for a couple of hours for the pellets to pass. 'I used a plastic bag as a glove to pull them out of the toilet bowl and throw them in the bathtub. I washed them and counted them. They were all there. And none of them had ripped.

'That's when it really hit me that what I had done was enormously risky. I handed over the bag filled with pellets to this fella, who insisted he really was a cousin of the lad I'd slept with back in Casablanca. He gave me an envelope with £3,000 cash in it and mentioned that he'd scribbled his mobile number on it as well and that I was to call him next time I wanted to do another run.

'More importantly, he said that my lad in Casablanca was desperate to see me. My heart melted. I was hooked in. I didn't really care if it was all a con to keep me onside. Just having those memories of what had just happened would keep me going for the moment. But I wanted more of him and more of that cash, so I could keep my family afloat.'

Jane has since been back twice to see her young lover and done a mule run each time. But she said that for the first time she was starting to have serious doubts about whether to return to Morocco ever again. She sensed her 'lad' was cooling on her. She explains: 'Last time I went over to do a mule run, he seemed much more cool and businesslike with me and it felt like he was just going through the motions when we slept together. Maybe that was a good thing because I knew that in reality I could never abandon my husband and kids for a Moroccan gigolo.'

But, Jane admits, giving up being a mule may not be as easy as she hopes. 'I've had daily calls from the lad in Morocco and his cousin here in Birmingham also won't stop phoning me. The lad says he loves me and wants me to visit him but he probably doesn't mean it. His cousin sounds much more threatening about everything and keeps saying, "You must go and see him and bring me back more hash." I don't like the tone of his voice but what can I do? I am a little afraid this man might tell my husband what has been happening and it will break his heart. I couldn't do that to him and the kids. They don't deserve any of this.'

But Jane is equally pragmatic about what might well

happen if she succumbs to the pressure and does another hash run. 'I'm a realist and I feel that eventually one of those bags will burst inside me, or someone in the Moroccan gang will inform on me to customs. I know they often do that with mules just to make the customs people stay off their backs the rest of the time.

'If a bag bursts inside me it might kill me. If I get arrested I'll end up in prison. So either way, I will lose my family and destroy them in the process. I know that the best thing to do is refuse to go on any more runs.' She hesitates for a moment. 'But then I think about him. His smile. His body. It's hard to resist when you have bugger all else to look forward to in your life.'

Meanwhile, Jane's husband has dipped into clinical depression so severely that when we next met she revealed that he had had to be coaxed down from the roof of a local shopping centre car park after threatening to jump. Jane seemed to have hardened to everything since our first meeting: 'He knows there is someone else in my life and it's literally killing him. I don't know what to do. I can't tell him the truth but I know I should split from him in the best way possible for the kids. However, neither of us can afford to be apart because of the expense of having separate homes. It's a horrible situation and it is entirely my fault.'

Jane admits that she often feels tempted to call her lover in Casablanca or his cousin. 'I know I'm only looking for an escape route from my responsibilities. I know I'm being a coward but worst of all, I know in my heart of hearts that

I'd probably end up dead or in prison if I agree to another mule run.'

With that, Jane looks at her watch. 'Shit. I'm going to be late picking up the kids from school. Back to reality, eh?'

CHAPTER 13

MICKY

East Londoner Micky, 29, used to deal cocaine, but he ended up snorting more than he was selling, breaking the golden drug-dealing rule – don't get high on your own supply. He deals hash these days because the money is good and the risk of a long prison term is not as great.

He explains: 'I had to stop dealing coke because I was getting seriously hooked. It's fine having the occasional joint but that white stuff does yer head in after a while. I was making stupid moves and taking big risks. I knew it was time to move to the softer stuff. Thank fuckin' God I did it before it was too late.'

Micky operates out of a swish apartment in a block close to Canary Wharf, in London's bustling Docklands area where the majority of the capital's bankers work and play. 'It's the perfect spot for this game. Most of these people do very stressful jobs and they like to unwind after a hard day at work and that's where I come in. It's always better to deal with rich bastards than poor, desperate types. The people round here treat me with respect and always show good manners. Some of them even buy me the occasional drink because they like to think I am their friend but first and foremost I am their dealer and I don't really want them to forget it.'

Micky has been introduced to me by a old-time villain I know called Teddy, who despite being almost eighty years of age, still enjoys the occasional puff on a joint as well as dipping into all the other traditional recreational drugs, such as cocaine and MDMA or ecstasy. When he first told me about Micky, Teddy was full of praise. 'He's a good lad. Never pushes his luck and he's not afraid to talk to someone like you.' Teddy tended to judge such characters on their ability to be a 'true professional' and he undoubtedly placed Micky in that category.

Micky himself comes from a long line of east London villains. His father was a chauffeur for the infamous 1960s London criminals, the Kray Twins. His uncle spent ten years in the slammer for armed robbery. But Micky is an altogether more reluctant villain, as he explains.

'I was brought up in the underworld but I always promised my mum I would avoid being a villain and do something useful with my life. She hated it all and was always trying to get my dad to get a so-called "proper job" but it never happened.'

Micky's first job after leaving school was as a clerk in a law firm in the City. He had high hopes that he'd end up being a trainee solicitor but things didn't quite turn out like that. 'I was a sharp kid and the lawyer I worked for knew that only too well. But I made a fatal error by pulling one of the clients, a savvy Essex bird who was up for fraud. She got off the charges eventually but I was given the axe for knocking her off. It was all most unfortunate.'

Micky says he then drifted into the cocaine business through a cousin. 'My dad would have killed me if he knew what I was up to because he was well aware that my mum would blame him for any criminality I was involved in. So I didn't tell anyone in my immediate family what I was up to.'

But after a number of near-death experiences and a lot of 'heavy pressure' from a gang of south London drug barons, Micky stepped back from the coke game for ever.

However, the switch to dealing in hash brought an altogether different list of complications. Micky explains: 'Hash is harder to smuggle because it is obviously bigger in size and it smells a hell of lot. When I first started dealing in it, I kept it stored in my flat but it stunk the place out and I had to find a lock-up with plenty of ventilation. In any case, it's madness to keep a lot of it in your own home.'

In a dark area at the back of that very same lock-up, Micky cuts up a '9 bar' (a slang term for a 9oz block of hash). He smokes a large joint as he works, carefully cutting down the large block into smaller deals, which he weighs on a set of small digital scales and then wraps in cellophane.

'I sell 10s and 20s – which is basically a sixteenth or an

eighth of an ounce. I have my customers and I deliver to them so no one knows where I live. You got to be careful and not be stupid.'

Micky travels carefully through the London streets and he always sticks to the speed limit. As he drives his mobile rings; it's another customer. He answers on the hands free so he doesn't get pulled over by the police. 'That's the other problem with hash. The coppers can smell it a mile away, so I only ever keep small quantities in the car and it's always very tightly wrapped in clingfilm.'

We cross the Thames to head through the mean streets of south-east London. It's not an area Micky normally frequents. 'This customer of mine has just moved to Blackheath and he likes big blocks of the stuff, so I make him my only across-the-river delivery. It's dangerous being out here. If you deal on other people's turf they come down on you like a ton of bricks. Lots of cowboys and quite a few Indians and I don't want to meet any of them.'

Micky eventually steers his Audi estate into the short driveway of a big, detached house just off the main A2 road down to the Channel ports. It's got to be worth £2 million in London's grossly over-inflated property market.

'Stay put,' says Micky, opening the lid of the armrest between us and removing a tightly wrapped ounce brick of hash. 'Won't be long.'

Micky then hops out of his car and shuts the door quietly, all in one neat movement. I watch as he climbs the steps to the dark-grey recently painted double front door.

HASH

A man opens it and greets Micky with a bear hug. Micky then walks inside the hallway and the front door closes behind him. Just then I notice through a big bay window a group of people sitting at a table; obviously the host is holding a dinner party.

Suddenly I spot the door to the dining room opening and a man leads Micky in. Then he is introduced to all of the guests. There must be at least a dozen people of all ages, sizes and shapes. Not one of them looks surprised to see him and then Micky plonks his tightly wrapped brick of hash on the table, smiles at everyone before turning casually towards the door and waving goodbye to the entire party.

Less than a minute later he is firing up his Audi for the journey back to Docklands. 'What a bunch of snotty-nosed prats. I hate it when a customer tries to show me off like that. The one good thing about coke was that when you dropped it off with a punter, they always tried to keep it hush-hush because, after all, it is an A-class narcotic. Bloody hash users think it's as normal as having a cup of tea.'

Micky reveals that his customers range from lawyers to film stars to builders. 'That's the thing about hash. It crosses the old class divide with a vengeance. Mind you, I wouldn't supply any old riff-raff with it 'cos that's asking for trouble.'

He says he always checks out his potential customers very carefully after they have been recommended to him. 'I leave nothing to chance. It only takes one punter to grass you up or to turn out to be an undercover cozzer [cop] and then you're fucked.'

And when it comes to his own supplies, Micky believes in the old saying 'Loose Lips Sink Ships' and refuses point blank to reveal any details about the gangsters who supply him with his hash, except to say: 'They'd have me topped if I started blabbering about them to anyone. They are the real thing – a right heavy mob. We might be talking about hash here but that doesn't stop the big names from wanting a chunk of the business.'

Just then I remembered something that his old crim pal Teddy had said about Micky before I even met him. 'Micky's in with the big boys. He likes to play the small-time hood but he's actually got his finger in a lot of pies.'

That comment makes me wonder who the real Micky is. Maybe he's fed me a lot of lies because, like many criminals, he fancies the fame but not if it costs him his business. But, as if he is reading my mind, Micky then chips in: 'What you see is what you get with me. I don't play any games and I think that's the key to my survival.'

'But,' I ask, 'how come you seem so untouchable compared with many others in the same game?'

Micky takes his time answering and the silence that envelops the car feels a tad awkward. Then he takes a long, deep breath. 'Listen. I like to think I am one of the clever ones. I know what side my bread is buttered on and I keep everyone happy, so that they never come down on me hard. If that makes me untouchable, so be it.' Then he hesitated for another brief moment. 'Let's just say I have the backing of certain people who no one in this game would ever dare try to cross. Does that make sense?'

I nod in tacit agreement, although if truth be known I was no nearer an answer to my question than five minutes earlier.

CHAPTER 14

PERRY AND DEV

Away from the chaotic high-risk, low-reward world of so-called amateur mules such as Jane, there are a number of highly specialised UK-based 'professionals' who make a good living smuggling small quantities of high-quality hash to a tightly knit, select band of customers.

I was introduced to Perry and Dev by one of Essex's most notorious criminals, a character known as Geordie, even though he does not come from the north-east of England. Geordie calls Perry and Dev his 'boys', which seems to imply they work for him but at no point during our interview am I able to actually confirm if they even have a boss.

Perry and Dev are what we used to call 'a couple of likely lads from Essex'. They're both in their late thirties and they seem like genuinely close friends, who are proud of the fact they watch each other's backs. They even went to school together.

But these two hash dealers are in a very different 'game' from the sort of characters I have so far encountered in the secret underworld of hash. They are what is known in the trade as 'do-it-yourself-merchants'. They buy their hash in Spain from one specific supplier. Then Perry 'mules' it over to the UK and they distribute it to their specialised customers. This is very unusual in the hash game because these two partners in crime have a small but select client base and claim they guarantee the quality of the hash in a way few other dealers could.

Perry comes from a broken home and a multi-racial background. He learned the tricks of the trade in approved school and reckons he hasn't looked back since. He's been involved in other forms of smuggling in the past but decided to set up this small high-grade hash smuggling operation because he was fed up with being ripped off by powerful villains in the criminal underworld of Essex.

Both Perry and Dev have spent time in prison for drug offences and it was after a long spell inside that Perry decided it was time they started working as a self-contained unit. He explains: 'I love hash myself and I like to think I am an expert at testing the stuff to make sure it is of the highest quality. That's why I am the one who does the mule run every month.'

Perry explains that he takes a budget airline flight into southern Spain – 'I use different airports so that no one flags me up' – once every calendar month. 'I try to turn it into a bit of mini-holiday. I mean, not many people can enjoy the sunshine and still earn a lot of dosh in the process, can they?'

But it's here that Perry's version of 'muling' turns out to be very different from the desperadoes willing to swallow potentially deadly pellets and wait for them to come out the other 'end'. Perry straps the tightly packed bricks of hash round his waist with extra strong tape. The hash itself is triple packed in cellophane so that it does not smell and then smothered in hair conditioner to put the sniffer dogs off the scent.

'A lot of other villains I know think I am barmy. But I tell you what? I've been doing this for five years and I've never even come close to being pulled.'

Perry believes it's all about front – confidence. He exudes it in bucketloads, so it's hard not to agree with him.

'I'm as calm as the proverbial cucumber. I never even break out in a sweat. I've got this routine when I arrive at the airport with the hash already strapped around me. I check in, then grab myself a beer to calm my nerves, then I swan off to the toilet and double check that nothing is sticking out too much, so to speak. Then I head for customs and bingo, I'm through . . . they don't even feel it if they pat me down after going through a scanner because I pack it extra tight and I always wear an extra sweatshirt under my T-shirt.'

Then, Perry proudly lifted his shirt to reveal he was wearing exactly what he'd just described. 'See? It works perfectly. I've never fancied swallowing the stuff and then shitting it out the other end. It's too risky. I'd rather take my chances with this routine. In any case, I can carry much more product than if I swallowed it.'

Perry then slowly and painstakingly unwraps the sticky tape wrapped around his waist and lower stomach. It sounds excruciating as the sticky side of the tape rips away at his body hair. 'This is the only problem. It bleedin' well hurts when you pull the tape off!'

Perry eventually lays out fifteen neatly packed bricks of hash on the table in front of him and I casually ask him the street value of what he has just smuggled through. 'They're worth two grand a brick so that makes thirty thousand, once we've sold it all to our customers.'

Then I dare to ask what Perry paid for the hash in Spain. 'Hundred and fifty quid a block. Not a bad little earner, eh?'

His quieter partner Dev chips in: 'Don't be too flashy, son. We don't want half the world thinking they can make good money out of hash.' For a split second Dev looks straight at Perry, who realises there is a serious undertone to his friend's voice.

'Yeah, but not many people have got the bottle to bring it in the way I do,' he adds proudly.

Dev looks happy. 'We're in this together and because we do everything ourselves the profits are healthy and everyone's happy, eh?'

Perry's not even listening because he's making his own joint with a tiny shred of hash he's peeled off the corner of a packet. 'I tell you, the quality of this smoke is the key to our success. We only provide the best, top-grade hash. It's vital because we're charging four times more than you'd pay in the local pub for some mucked about crap that's probably no more than 40 per cent genuine hash.'

Perry's sucking in a big mouthful of hash smoke as his partner Dev continues: 'The great thing about selling top-quality hash in these parts is that only the rich punters can afford it and they are such keen aficionados that they are charming to deal with and treat us with the utmost respect. There is none of that diving in and out of shitty tower block apartments filled with scum merchants. No, the majority of our customers live in houses with long driveways. That's the way we like to keep it, too.'

With that Perry and Dev finish off the bottles of beer they've been supping throughout the interview and announce plans to head off with their hash to do some 'drop-offs'. They don't invite me along but then, as Dev puts it: 'There's no way we're going to upset our customers for you.'

Perry then chips in: 'You could call us the Harrods of hash suppliers. And as long as we keep going this way, we should keep safe and very rich!'

With that, they gathered up their produce, dropped it carefully into a backpack and headed off to the Kawasaki motorbike they preferred to use when selling their hash in the badlands of Essex.

That's when I recall how Perry said a few minutes earlier that Dev was the only person in the world he trusts and that I then caught a glimpse between them and realise their bond is the key to their survival.

CHAPTER 15

TOM

There are still a few old-time 'heads' in the hash business – the self-confessed old hippies convinced that selling hash is no more illegal than running a wine bar and that their posh English accent virtually gives them the right to sing hash's praises.

Ex-public schoolboy Tom, from Berkshire, in the south of England, is proud of his 'expert' knowledge of hash. He firmly believes that it has helped him hold onto a loyal set of customers, who only ever buy hash from him.

'I don't deal and have never dealt in anything other than hash. Coke and ecstasy is heavy stuff and I don't want to be responsible for anything that might happen to the health of my customers,' he says. 'I'm a professional hash dealer full stop. I make a decent living out of it because I am trusted. I'm also a typical old hippy who believes that because hash comes from the ground it is healthy for people. There is nothing chemical in the hash I sell and I think that puts me head and shoulders above everyone else in this game.'

Tom says hash has provided him with a healthy income for more than thirty years. He claims to have numerous celebrity clients whom he regularly visits in London and says he is often flown across continents with hash for tycoon customers who live outside the UK. 'My business relies solely on word of mouth. The rich and sometimes famous people I supply put a good word in to their chums and that word gets around.' He adds proudly: 'D'you know? I've got at least ten customers whom I've supplied throughout the thirty years I've been in this business. I reckon that's pretty unique.'

Two weeks before we met, Tom even flew out to Tibet to inspect a shipment of the finest Himalayan before it was smuggled into Europe. 'I like to make these sorts of visits because it keeps my suppliers on their toes. I pride myself on this sort of personal service and I'd soon start losing my customers if I let the quality slide.'

The trip to Tibet was paid for by a rich client, who happens to be a member of one of the world's most famous banking families. 'He just called me up one day and said he wanted ten grand's worth of Himalayan and he'd be happy to cover all my travel costs to go out there and make sure it was of the highest quality. I was happy to oblige.'

This is where Tom is different from most other members of the secret underworld of hash that I encountered while researching this book. He operates in broad daylight without any pretence about what he does. He firmly believes that by being so open he, in effect, is protecting himself from any trouble. He explains: 'I am who I am. I think by being open and letting my business speak for itself in an organic sense I am not perceived as a threat to anyone. By that I mean criminals and the police. They're not interested in people like me. I'm just a hard-working businessman selling produce that any adult should have the right to consume. Don't get me wrong. I don't want hash to be made legal because then the price would come down and I'd soon be out of business! No, I think the way it is now in the UK suits me fine. The police are more interested in catching the coke barons and I'm considered a bit of a harmless old eccentric providing a service to responsible adults. Simple as that.'

Tom's voice veers from a soft mid-Atlantic right-on hippy drawl to an upper-crust public school accent, depending on what he is talking about and whether he is puffing on a joint. But it is clear he has few worries in the world and enjoys his 'job' immensely. 'I get real job satisfaction because I am proud of my produce and a lot of my customers have become my friends. I get to fly all over the world at other people's expense. What more could you want?'

Tom's base is in a small coastal town with a good rail connection to London. His waterside apartment is filled with classic furniture and knick-knacks brought back from his numerous trips abroad. Rugs from Morocco. Hash pipes from India. Buddhas from Thailand. Turbans from Afghanistan.

While we are chatting he brings out four small bags, each containing a different colour and texture of hash. He pulls each small brick out and smells one at a time as he tells me where it has come from and why it is popular with certain customers.

'Take this hash from Afghanistan. It's mellow to smoke and slides down your throat like velvet but it's got an amazing kick-in about thirty seconds after you inhale it. I recommend it for people who've got all day on their hands because once you get stuck into this stuff, you'll barely be able to walk.'

Then he pulls out a much darker slab of hash. 'This is Indian. It's much gentler and many of my business clients like it because they can snatch a toke between meetings and still operate on a "normal" level. They say it makes them more relaxed for presentations and stuff like that.'

Tom lives with his twenty-seven-year-old Latvian girlfriend, despite having a wife and three children living nearby. 'I told you I was a typical old hippy at heart. Free love and all that. I still look after my wife and kids but I can't handle living with them.'

And unlike many of the other members of the secret underworld of hash, Tom says his wife and children as well as other friends and relatives all know what he does for a living. 'Why should I hide it from them? I consider myself to be the ultimate hash professional. I am proud of what I do.'

But what about his children? Would he mind if one of them ended up in the same 'profession'?

Tom sits back, takes another suck on his joint and then answers: 'That's a tricky one because I really want them to be doctors and lawyers and stuff like that. If they screw up their exams and don't get into university like I did then maybe being in the hash business might be their best choice. But first of all I want them to try and make it in the "real" world.'

Tom's backstory provides a fascinating insight into the so-called 'acceptable face of drug dealing' in the UK in the twenty-first century. He has carefully nurtured an image as an above-board character with nothing to hide and that has undoubtedly helped his business continue to thrive.

But surely, I ask him, there have been a few problems with suppliers along the way? Tom smiles somewhat more nervously than earlier. 'Now that's a good question. My customers simply don't want to know about the "other" side of this business. I actually think they like to imagine that I only ever deal with nice, smiley-smiley farmers who give me a hug and slab of hash and then we're on our way. Well, of course that is utter bollocks.

'I have to deal with some really horrible characters sometimes and it's the one side of this game that I loathe. One time I tried to get a millionaire customer to agree to finance me for a year, so I could set up a complete supply chain in order to avoid the troublesome criminal elements but he chickened out in case I ever got arrested. Shame because I'd love nothing more than to control my supply of hash from start to finish.'

So who are these gangsters he deals with? 'They're the guys in the middle. The ones who shift the hash from the back of beyond to the UK. Without them this stuff would not be sitting here in front of us today. Sad but true. And the only problem with supplying such a vast range of hash is that I have to deal with a different set of gangsters for each "brand". There is a bunch of Turks out of north London who smuggle the best hash from Afghanistan. There's a team of west London Sikhs bringing in the hash from Nepal and there is a gang of French mafia importing the majority of my hash from Morocco.

'It's when I deal with these people that I really earn my money. They are mainly erratic, paranoid characters, often with trigger-brain tempers. I usually make sure I'm stoned when I meet them because then I stay calm and there is less risk of winding them up. But only the other day, one of the Turks lost his rag with me and stuck a gun in my face because he thought I was trying to avoid paying him.

'I fronted it out with him because you cannot ever show them you are scared otherwise they will start bullying you and ripping you off. The funny thing is that the really heavy characters don't really know how to handle me because I don't fit into the usual stereotype of a dope dealer. It actually gives me a bit of an advantage over them just so long as they don't think I am looking down my nose at them.'

Tom admits that at one time in the late 1990s he got involved in buying hash through one of the UK's most notorious criminal families, based in north-west London. 'That was a nightmare because the police were after them for murders and coke deals and stuff like that. I had no idea at first I was actually dealing with this particular gang because they used an associate to cover their tracks. It was only when I spotted this bloke in a club in the West End with the oldest brother of this fearsome family crew. His face had been plastered all over the newpapers only a few days earlier in connection with a hitman killing. I somehow managed to pull away from them, even though they tried to put enormous pressure on me to continue buying my hash through them.

'I wriggled out of it by saying I thought I was being watched by the local police. Somehow they swallowed it and we parted ways reasonably amicably, although I remain convinced to this day that if I ever bumped into those characters again they'd probably beat me up just for the sake of it. People like that hate to even suspect they have been conned. They think it's bad for their reputation.'

Tom then paused for a moment while taking another toke. His girlfriend Maria appeared at the bedroom door sleepy eyed and with a silky dressing gown barely covering her body. Tom looked up smiling. 'Shall I tell him about those Croatians, baby?'

Maria shrugged her shoulders. 'Yeah, sure. Why not?'

Tom sucked what remained out of his joint and then dropped it in a huge onyx ashtray on the coffee table in front of him.

'This country is turning into a bloody cesspit filled with eastern Europeans,' says Tom. 'And they all think they have the right to muscle in on businesses like mine. Only a couple of weeks ago, I got a call from some foreign-sounding chappie who claimed he wanted to buy some hash off me. I don't usually take new callers but this guy mentioned a mutual acquaintance, so I told him to come round. Well, he turned out to be a right nasty piece of work from Croatia and he arrived with two meathead friends. They sat down here calm as anything at first and told me they had a proposition to make to me. I could see what was coming from a mile away but I sat there and listened politely all the same. In reality though, I just wanted them out of the front door pronto.

'Anyway, this one guy spoke in very fluent English and told me that he was going to supply all my hash to me and I was going to give him 50 per cent of all my takings. It was a classic. They actually thought they could just come in here and take over my business. I guess it was a bit like the Krays in the 1960s taking over a pub and telling the landlord who owned it that if he objected he'd end up in a rubbish tip some place or inside a car which had been crushed at a scrap metal yard.

'Well, I knew I had to tread gently with these guys so I told the Croatian frontman that I'd be delighted to consider his generous offer and would he please give me forty-eight hours to get things into order, so I could make all the necessary arrangements. This guy looked at me like I was bonkers. I reckon he was expecting me to object on the spot and then his two sidekicks could shove a gun in my face. Well, I haven't survived this long by being completely stupid.

'The moment they left, I contacted my Turkish suppliers in north London and told them that a bunch of Croatians were trying to take over my business. They hit the roof because Turks hate Croatians. My Turkish friend immediately volunteered to take care of them. I didn't hear another thing about what happened to the Croatians but they never came knocking on my door ever again.'

So. Even 'gentle old hippies' like Tom had to occasionally resort to violence in order to survive in the secret underworld of hash. In some ways it was quite a relief to hear that, after all, he was no different from any of the others.

Tom predicts an uncertain future for the UK underworld. 'Soon it's going to be crawling with so many bloody foreigners that the police are going to lose control and it will be back like living in the Victorian times with crooks and pimps on every street corner trying to make a quid. A lot of these people from abroad are much more desperate and hungry for cash than the Brits. The cities will soon be overflowing with them and that's when the real problems will begin. I'm just hoping I will be safely retired and living on some Caribbean island by then with a joint in one hand and a lovely fair maiden in the other.'

CHAPTER 16

ON THE STREETS LEN

Street dealers in hash have two clear priorities – easy money and personal autonomy. Though they do face risks other people struggle to relate to, if a dealer conducts himself well and quits while he's ahead, he might avoid the law or a knife in the gut.

Take ex-Marine Len. He is living proof that whatever class of hash dealer you happen to be, it will fuck you up one way or the other. Len was a hash dealer from the age of fifteen until he joined up and then when he bailed out of the services three years ago, he simply started up in the 'business' once again.

Len says it all began when he bought his first baggie of hash as a schoolboy, in his hometown of Newcastle: 'I bought it and flipped it for double the price to someone else,' he says. These days, Len has a professional pride in his product. He even insists that he always tries his hash before he sells it to anyone. 'I don't want anyone to get sick on my supply,' he says.

Len is even careful about not spending his hash cash in big amounts. 'That would flag me up as someone dodgy and I'd soon get a pull,' he explains.

Len claims that many former soldiers have ended up dealing in drugs because 'there is nothing for them when they get out. No one cares about you so it's hardly surprising many of us end up flogging gear.' But Len provides a fascinating insight into his 'profession'. He claims one of the biggest misconceptions about hash smokers is that they are all middle class and he is certainly living proof of it. Len works on the gritty streets of west London where he visits pubs and clubs on virtually a nightly basis in order to sell hash to his hardcore of customers, virtually all of whom are either unemployed or working in menial, poorly paid jobs.

Len calls his hash 'pub grub' because, he says, that is what it is. 'Buying a lump of hash is no different from ordering a pint or buying a packet of fags these days,' says Len. 'In fact, it's often a lot cheaper.'

Len openly admits his hash is cut with other ingredients to 'stretch it out' in order to maximise profits. But he even has a pet theory as to why that doesn't seem to matter at his end of the hash game. 'People just want to know they're having a smoke. If it turns out that the lump they've just sprinkled in a ciggie consists of 50 per cent tree bark they don't really seem to care. It's all about the ritual. Buying the hash off me, ripping open a ciggie, spreading the tobacco out on a paper and then crumbling the hash into it. People love the idea they are doing something naughty, something illegal.'

Len provides £10 and £20 bags of hash to more than 200 regular customers. He reckons his high earnings are down to quantity, not quality. 'Oh, I've heard all the crap down the years from the so-called "posh end" of this business. They talk about hash as if it's some kind of art form. It's a drug, simple as that. And I'm a drug dealer who makes a good living out of it.'

After meeting Len at his home twenty miles south of London, we head out to the west of the city for one of his 'drop-offs'. He explains: 'There aren't many places I'd let you come with me but this boozer we are going to is wall to wall with spliff merchants and they don't seem to give a toss who I walk in with.'

Len is right. As we wander into the nondescript pub close to a noisy dual carriageway, no one seems remotely interested. Len jokes under his breath: 'Stupid fuckers. They're all so stoned in here they can barely remember who I am.'

We go to the main bar and order two drinks before a middle-aged man with a beer belly and a bright red face approaches. Len immediately recognises him and the two of them walk to a darkened corner at the other end of the bar. Less than a minute later Len is back alongside me.

'He buys two twenty-quid bags off me at least four times a week. Now those sort of regular customers I love! If I had two hundred of them on the go at any one time, I'd be rich enough to retire from this game within a year.'

But, Len admits, a lot of customers come and go. 'It's hardly a seasonal business but sometimes I think that's how it feels. A lot of my customers are such stoners that I think half of them lose my phone number. That's the other reason why I pop into pubs like this. It reminds people who I am in case they are so off their heads they've forgotten! I am being serious here.'

We sup our two halves of cider gently while Len's eyes snap around the bar just to make sure none of his old customers have shown up. 'It's quiet in here today. Maybe they're all at home sleeping off that last lot of hash I flogged 'em.'

Just then, a much younger man in his early twenties walks in. He looks straight at Len and nods. Len moves alongside the man. Then the two of them walk outside.

Three or four minutes later, Len reappears with a broad grin on his face. 'Blimey. You'll wish you'd put a tape recorder in my pocket when you hear this, mate.'

I nod to encourage him to proceed.

'That kid was working as a "rep" for a copper, who wanted four twenty-quid bags. What a result!'

'What's a "rep"?' I ask, almost innocently.

'That's a middle man. He was coming in on behalf of the copper.'

'But how did he find you?'

'I'm known in these parts.'

But, I wanted to know, why didn't the policeman deal direct with Len?

'Oh, I get this sort of stuff all the time. Coppers don't want to be spotted talking to anyone like me so they use other people to do their dirty work for them. Typical slippery bastards, eh?'

'But how d'you know he was working for a policeman then?'

'Oh I know 'cos I asked him. I never flog stuff to people without knowing exactly who I am speaking to. It's one of my golden rules.'

'Yeah,' I point out. 'But what's the point in that cop using that young guy if you now know who he is?'

'That's their problem, ain't it?'

Our conversation was interrupted by a text coming through on Len's smart phone. He stopped to read it.

'Right. We're on our way. One of my special customers wants a drop-off,' said Len, laughing mainly to himself. He did a lot of that.

Fifteen minutes later, I'm sitting in Len's rundown Vauxhall estate car as he knocks on the door of a third-floor council flat on one of the biggest estates in west London. It's an area fraught with deprivation; gangs of feral kids out on the narrow walkways that divide half a dozen tower blocks. Older youths congregating on street corners.

I glance up at the doorway that Len has just entered and wonder what he's doing there. It's another twenty minutes until he emerges, by which time a pack of local youths have started circling Len's vehicle as if I am an undercover police officer.

It's only when they see Len's obese figure waddling towards them that they pull back. He gives them a cold, hard stare.

Back inside the car, Len lets out a long, irritable breath. 'What a fuckin' shit-hole. You're lucky I didn't take you in there, mate.'

Len continued without bothering to let me respond: 'That is what you call a drug den. It's horrible and smelly and he's got a family of Rottweilers who bare their teeth and then try to stick their noses up yer arse. I told him it puts the punters off but he doesn't seem to give a fuck. Silly old bastard.'

It then transpires that the 'silly old bastard' is a sixty-seven-year-old coke dealer called Stevie, who buys all his hash from Len. 'He says he hates coke so he needs the hash to stay nice and calm for his customers,' explains Len.

Stevie runs his stinking drugs den out of an empty council flat which, according to Len, is often the way with coke and crack dealers. 'That stuff's all about the quick hits and dealers move into an empty place for a couple of months and then move on to a new den. The key for them is to hit everyone within close range. I've seen queues of more than a dozen desperate crackheads waiting to get into his den.'

Len says he turned his back on Class A drug dealing long ago. 'I stick to hash because it's nice and solid work if you can get it. Just sitting in Stevie's drug den is enough to put you off crack and coke for life. It's a complete shit-hole and there's also the risk that some bastard will try and muscle you out of the way eventually.'

Len says that Stevie is 'shot to shit' and barely able to thread a sentence together 'until he has a toke'. He explains: 'Poor bastard has snorted so much shit over the years that he's only just capable of running that den. I'm sure someone younger and more trigger happy will pay him a visit sooner rather than later.'

Back in Len's car, we don't have to travel far from the estate to find ourselves in the middle of one of London's richest property areas. Len's mood lifts almost immediately. 'This is where I wish all my customers came from. You don't get any trouble from the middle classes but then again they don't take as many drugs. It's what I call a bit of a Catch-22, eh?'

Len says he prefers to be 'on the road' selling hash rather than dealing out of a specific location 'because it's harder for the law to nab me red-handed'.

He went on to explain some of the other golden rules of his business: 'I don't keep my stash at home, ever. I take the dog out for a walk and then hide it under a bush or near a tree. It's always packed airtight so no water can get into it but it's vital it's not at home just in case the cozzers come calling.'

Len continued: 'I've been chased down a few times by the law and I always chuck the produce anywhere I know I can come back the next day and recover it. One time I threw it on a roof when the police pulled me as I was walking along a street. They didn't have a clue about it and next day I got a ladder and clambered up and got it back. Another time I had to throw my stash in a pond when I spotted a couple of plain-clothes coppers behind me in a park one day. I came back later with a long pole and fished it out.'

Len says he has no qualms about people who smoke too much hash. 'It's a free world, ain't it? If they want to smoke themselves silly then it's up to them. I don't judge people like that. I'm not forcing them to smoke the stuff, am I? People need to take responsibility for their own actions. I know hash can fuck people up but the way I look at it is that they were probably fucked up before they even took their first ever puff of a joint.'

Then Len made a surprising confession; he often uses lines of cocaine to 'keep going' when out and about delivering hash to his customers. 'I know it might sound strange to most potheads but coke is great at helping me stay alert during a long day in this game. It's funny 'cos a lot of people who smoke hash really frown upon coke users. Personally, I don't see the difference. They're all drugs that give you a high of some sort. I need cocaine to keep me alert and it really does the trick but isn't it daft that I can't admit that to my customers in case it puts them off me?'

Len reckons he makes in the region of £2,000 a week as a street-level hash dealer. But he openly admits he hasn't put much aside for a rainy day. 'I'm the idiot who spends all his cash. It's madness really 'cos one day this whole game will go down the tube for me and then I'll be like most of my mates and joining the nation's unemployed. I keep telling myself I should save some cash but I've got another weakness that sucks up much of my hard-earned money – gambling.'

Len confesses that he loses up to £1,500 a week in betting shops, gambling mainly on horses. 'It's a bigger weakness than drugs in my book. I wish I could knock it on the head but I enjoy the buzz. But it really is a mug's game and as long as I am hooked I need to sell hash to survive.'

Len's favourite customer is Ben, a fifty-two-year-old ex-army officer from Surrey, who was shot and almost killed on duty in a war zone more than twenty years ago. Now he uses hash to help ease the pain of his injuries. Len says Ben knows he's helping finance criminality but his need for hash is indisputable.

'The guy is a real gem, an army hero who put his life on the line for the rest of us. This is a funny old game,' says Len. 'You get a huge cross-section of customers because hash is probably the most classless drug in the world and long may it be that way.'

CHAPTER 17

CYRIL

Career criminals adore the drugs industry because it's all about 'the product'. So says Cyril, probably one of the most unlikely hash barons you'll ever meet. He lives in a large five-bed detached mansion hidden away down an 800-yard drive in the middle of the Kent countryside. Cyril might come from the East End's school of hard knocks but he revels in living the life of a country squire.

Cyril is a hash 'financier'. He never gets his hands dirty by even touching the hash as it journeys through the underworld before ending up being smoked by Britain's millions of hash users. 'I hate the fuckin' stuff,' says Cyril drily and there is no doubt he is telling the truth. 'Why the hell would anyone take drugs? It beats me.'

Hash is just a lucrative business commodity to Cyril. He is a grandfather now and pledges that if any of his grandchildren got hooked on the stuff, 'I'd give 'em a good clip round the ear.' Cyril doesn't really seem to appreciate the irony of that statement.

Everything he does centres around money. 'If there's an earner in it for me, I'll do it,' he says. Cyril's been 'in and out' of the hash game for more than thirty years. He first got involved in the trade after spending eighteen months in prison for fraud. 'Prison. That's where you learn the truth about drugs. I made more connections in the slammer than anywhere else and when I got out I knew hash was the business I was going to concentrate on. It's such a big earner.'

Cyril has a 'previous' history in money laundering and financial fraud but, he says, the beauty of being a drug baron is that he doesn't even have to 'touch the fuckin' stuff'.

He explains: 'The way I operate, the hash comes in to my boys and then gets pushed straight out again to the next rung on the ladder. Usually, it's not around for more than a few days in one of my lock-ups. The less time the better because that's when you'll get sent down if the Old Bill show up.'

Cyril's background was originally in watch and diamond dealing before he turned to crime. 'I had a shop in the City. It was the seventies and business was shit back then. I couldn't afford to keep it all going because the rent was astronomical. Then I met this bloke who said that I should use my accountant's qualifications to go into money laundering.'

When that eventually landed him in jail he switched to hash. Today, Cyril reckons hash provides him with 'about

70 per cent of my total earnings. It's a solid market. It doesn't change much but I like that because it means I know precisely what I am going to earn from each shipment.'

Cyril was reluctant to go into details about how the shipments of hash come into his hands because 'there are some evil bastards out there who'd soon try to take over my operation.'

But he did say: 'Just 'cos it's hash doesn't mean there aren't some bad villains involved in smuggling the stuff. My role is to cough up £50k on a Monday to pay for it and by Friday get £120k back no questions asked. That's a sweet deal as far as I am concerned.

'If I end up having to store it for longer that's obviously a bit of a pain but I have got a brilliant location to keep it for a few days if need be.'

Cyril then showed his true criminal colours when I ask him about what happens if his shipment 'goes walkabout'. He explains: 'That's happened a couple of times and I've had to make sure that those responsible for it have paid me back what was owed on the shipment. I don't care what their excuse is. They have to take financial responsibility for that shipment. It's one of the rules of this game. And if anyone fails to pay me back after a shipment is lost or stolen or confiscated by the cozzers then they are in deep shit. That's the way it goes in this business.'

Hearing Cyril talking about 'hurting' other gangsters brings the whole hash game back down to earth. His cold, ruthless attitude reminds me that hash remains just another illegal drug which gangsters like Cyril are making fortunes out of. As he himself admitted: 'Just because it's not Class A it doesn't mean the stakes aren't high. This is a criminal enterprise and like all such operations it has to make everyone a lot of money or else it's not worth doing.'

Cyril invited me to go in his gleaming black Bentley Turbo to a nearby lock-up garage, which he admitted is his 'centre of operations'. He explains: 'That'll sound like a joke when I show you this place but it's come in very handy down the years, especially when I've had a few problems with some villains who tried to double-cross me.'

Cyril opens the lock-up with an electronic remote control and the door slides up slowly to reveal three chairs, a table and a line of tools ranging from hacksaws to hammers hanging on the wall at the end of the garage. 'Welcome to my office,' says Cyril, almost proudly. 'This is where all the important meetings take place.'

Cyril walks over to a cupboard in the corner of the damp lock-up with its bare breeze-block walls and reaches up to get something from above the cupboard. As he turns to show me what is in his hand I see it is a black revolver.

'Don't worry. It's not loaded. I'm just looking after it for a friend.'

Then Cyril placed it carefully back where he got it from and continued his guided tour. 'See these tools?' says Cyril. 'They come in very handy if I think anyone is pulling my leg about something serious like a lost shipment of hash.'

Are you serious? I ask. 'Yeah. Why not? But I got to admit

when my associates see them hanging there they soon get the message. The last thing I want to resort to is actual violence. Much better to scare them shitless.'

In many ways Cyril is one of the single most dangerous criminals I had come across in my journey through the secret underworld of hash. He was dressed up to look like a perfectly normal middle-class businessman from Kent while in fact he was more capable of having someone killed than anyone else I had encountered.

As if reading my mind, Cyril then chipped in: 'Violence, or the threat of violence, is part of my business. If the other "team" isn't shit-scared of me, then I'm going to have a problem on my hands. I call it good PR, that's Public Relations to you and me. I want those villains out there to know they mustn't risk crossing me. Then I can be certain that things will go smoothly for every deal.'

Cyril leaned across and pulled a hacksaw off its perch and ran his fingertip slowly down the outside of the blade. 'See that?' he says, picking something out from between the tiny metal teeth.

'That's blood.' He laughed. 'That's what I always tell them and more often than not they look shit-scared and can't wait to get out of there in one piece.'

'Is it really?' I ask.

'No comment,' says Cyril with a hearty laugh.

Then he puts the hacksaw back in its place and picks up a claw hammer. 'My old London robber mates used to say that whacking a hammer on someone's fingernails usually did the trick after a few swings. It's also hard to prove because of the sort of injury you can inflict.'

Cyril couldn't resist then smashing the hammer down on the wooden surface of a worktop. It left an enormous dent about the size of a 50p piece. 'That's what it does to people's faces. Leaves them with a lasting reminder of who you are.'

'All this seems a bit old fashioned,' I say to Cyril.

'Bollocks. This sort of stuff always does the trick if a problem needs solving.'

A couple of minutes later Cyril flicks the remote to close the doors of the lock-up and we walk back to his Bentley.

With not a trace of irony in his voice, Cyril explains to me: 'I don't want you making out I am some sort of nutty psycho who gets people topped if they upset me. This is the trade I work in. I am a businessman and hash is a lucrative way for me to earn a living. End of story.'

CHAPTER 18

THE CONSULTANT

UK growers of cannabis plants have recently begun producing hash as well as grass as vast plantations of marijuana are cultivated in so-called 'home grows' throughout the country. Often they are in respectable suburban properties and the smartest family homes.

Between 2004 and 2007, British police detected around 800 cannabis 'grows' per year in the UK. This had risen to 7,000 by 2009/10, with the largest concentrations located in West Yorkshire, Greater Manchester and the West Midlands. A total of 750,000 cannabis plants were recovered by the police that year. The Association of Chief Police Officers estimates that home-grown cannabis now makes up around 70 to 80 per cent of the UK's commercial supply.

And it is not just the police that the army of illegal growers should fear. 'Home grows' have become so widespread that energy companies calculate that up to £100 million of electricity is being stolen to fuel the sophisticated lighting systems needed to encourage the drug to grow. British Gas – now a major supplier of electricity – has formed a special team to tackle the hash barons after detecting an upsurge in the use of power-draining hydroponic equipment to produce marijuana indoors without soil by pumping nutrients directly into the roots of the plants.

In Greater Leys, near the city of Oxford, two neighbourhood police officers delivering a stray letter to an address, stumbled across a cannabis factory at the house. Sergeant Ian Roch and Special Constable Oscar Hayward had been greeted by a 'strong smell' when they knocked on the door of the property. When two 'wide-eyed, scared people' answered the door their suspicions heightened. Amazingly, the two men managed to escape the clutches of the two officers, who then found sixty saplings, forty-five 2ft plants close to harvest and forty other 2ft plants.

Meanwhile, police in Newcastle called to a suspected burglary in 2011 discovered a huge cannabis farm in a house. Some 300 high-potency cannabis plants were seized, with an estimated street value of more than £150,000.

With average prices of £21 per quarter ounce, there is an ever growing commercial and personal market for home-produced hash in the UK.

That's where 'The Consultant' comes in . . .

I'll call him Tig because his real nickname is so memorable he's convinced he'll be recognised by all and sundry. Being unmasked could cost him dearly.

Tig is a UK-based freelance pot-growing expert, who actually bills himself as 'The Consultant' and specialises in organising every aspect of what he professionally calls a 'home-grown operation'. This can include everything from the renting of a suitable house to organising the heating, the lighting and, most important of all, the right crop to grow. Tig's 'clients' cover the whole gamut from people wanting to smoke their own cannabis to those who see it as a way to make a living. As a result, Tig's services do not come cheap.

Tig 'The Consultant' charges a flat fee of £3,000 for organising the setting up of growing rooms, sometimes in an otherwise empty rented house or one where the occupants have vacated at least an entire floor to make way for cannabis plants.

'It's a thriving business because growing here in the UK is a hell of a lot safer than importing cannabis from abroad,' says Tig. 'There is a general misconception that the quality of the stuff is inferior on home grows, but if the right buds are used with the right equipment you can match anything coming out of the mountains of Tibet or the paddy fields of Thailand. My job is to ensure that every single available inch in a house is used to grow the finest quality weed.'

Tig clearly loves his work and describes every assignment as 'a real challenge'.

He enthusiastically explains: 'I love it because, quite frankly, most of the people who try to get started don't have a clue how to do it properly. They need a character like me to kick off their home-grown production.'

Recently, Tig has made it his 'duty' to encourage home-grow operators to produce hash as well as grass. 'God knows why this hasn't been done before but it could effectively double the profit from every cannabis plant,' he explains. 'It suddenly dawned on me last year that I had been missing a trick with this home-grown thing for years. Hash is there. You just have to know how to get it out of the buds that are left over.

'It's as if people have been so obsessed with growing and selling their own potent weed they've overlooked the bloody obvious, which is that you can produce hash from what remains of those same plants.'

Tig says that all home growers need to do is follow his guide: 'Get the trim and buds off what remains after you've removed the grass and dry it all carefully. Then put it in the freezer for a couple of days. Take it out and grind it up into tiny particles of powder. Use a clean dustbin and add your trim and buds into the bin and then attach a thin netting around the edge of the bin.

'Then turn the bin upside down so the buds fall onto the net then shake the bin to make the remains of the buds turn into powder and keep filtering it at the same time. Then add the powder into either plastic or clingfilm and compress the powder very tightly. Then wrap it all up in paper. Add water and put it in the oven for twelve to seventeen minutes. Then use something solid like a rolling pin or hammer and press down on the hash, put it back in the freezer for fifteen minutes and you then have the hash.'

Tig considers himself both a hash and a grass consultant and believes that his income could triple over the next two or three years 'once people cotton on to the fact they can make double the crop from each plant'.

Tig epitomises the sort of characters who end up at this level in the secret underworld of hash. He's a happy-go-lucky fellow with an optimistic outlook on life, even though he's had some very close shaves during his career as a hash consultant.

He explains: 'I know this sounds kinda corny but I like helping people set up these sorts of operations here in the UK. Sure, I like the money too but I genuinely get a kick from seeing this sort of home-grown operation work out.'

The phrase 'home grown' is confusing because the sort of people who pay Tig for his expertise are often either criminal gangs or people who have hit on such hard times that they have turned to crime to make a living. Tig makes out he is some kind of pot-growing guru but in reality he is also a businessman with a very lucrative 'skill' to offer people.

Tig himself is an eccentric former public schoolboy who grew up surrounded by 'duckers and divers' including his own father, who sold second-hand cars. 'Sure, I didn't get a lot of grounding in basic morals but I learned how to survive and in many cases thrive, so I can't complain,' he says now.

For some years back in the early 1980s, Tig was an old-fashioned grass dealer in one of the richest areas of London: Kensington and Chelsea. Through his dealing, he says he got to know pop stars, actors and even a couple of members of the royal family as his reputation as a trustworthy supplier of the finest grass spread around west London.

Tig only 'fell into' the consultancy game some years later when he tried a bit of home growing when his supplies from abroad slowed down. He explains: 'I started doing a bit of home growing and was selling it on but it was nothing big. Just a few customers here and there. Then this twenty-two-year-old guy I was selling grass to asked me if I knew how to set up a proper home-grow operation because his mother had lost her job and they needed to find a way to make decent money very quickly, to pay the rent on their house.

'I moved into this guy's house and within three days we had converted the entire loft into a home-growing plantation. I chose the seeds and provided a lighting kit made from things you can buy at any DIY store. Within a couple of months the first crop of home-grown had been produced.'

Tig doesn't like to talk in any detail about his methods because he believes that 'might be bad for business'. 'The key is to buy the best cannabis seeds. Or they can even come out of your own grass supply. The aim is to germinate those seeds. That means dropping the seeds into moist soil. Place a group of them between about six moist paper towels, or in the pores of a moist sponge. Leave the towels or sponge moist but not soaking wet. Some weed seeds will germinate in twenty-four hours while others may take several days or even a week. Then you know you're in business.

'Next you have to plant the sprouts. As soon as a seed cracks open and begins to sprout, place it on some moist soil and sprinkle a little soil over the top of it. That's when you need to supply the plants with light. Fluorescent lights are the best. Hang them within two inches of the soil and keep them there even after the plants appear above the ground. But to ensure prime quality and the highest yield in the shortest time period, however, you need the help of a consultant like me . . .'

Tig is immensely proud of his skills as a 'consultant'. 'Those people I first worked for paid me a flat fee and then offered to pay me more for every visit I made to the loft to inspect the crop and make sure it was all growing properly. That made me realise there was a whole new market out there that needed the sort of advice I could offer.'

Within months, Tig had half a dozen 'consultancy' jobs on the go. 'It was amazing how many people wanted to set up a home-grow operation. Many of them wanted to sell on the weed but some were doing it purely for themselves. Quite frankly, I couldn't see anything wrong with it. I mean surely it's better to do it this way in the UK then line the pockets of cold-blooded gangsters who charge a fortune to smuggle stuff here?'

Tig himself says he has had a few run-ins with such criminals in the past, so he was delighted to find himself offering an 'advice service' to people 'who on the whole were just decent middle-class folk either with money problems or a serious pot habit'.

He explains: 'There has always been a clear demarcation line between weed smokers and those who prefer hash. I reckon that's why it's taken so long to wake up to the concept of using the remains of each plant to produce hash as well. I must be stupid not to have thought of it before but then again, neither did anyone else.'

Meanwhile, Tig tries his hardest to avoid the heavyweight home-grow criminals. 'I can't handle the Chinese and Vietnamese, who have started setting up entire rented houses filled with home-grown in recent years. They don't care about the quality and most of the people they have working in these houses are virtual slaves. It's a horrible side of the business which I do not want any part of.'

Tig is just the wrong side of fifty but he looks slim and fit. 'I love a decent smoke but I've always been very careful to look after myself as well. In any case, I have to be super alert in this job.'

He went on to explain: 'I am very wary of calls that come out of the blue asking me to help set up home-growing factories. Recently some Irish guy contacted me and offered me three times my normal fee to fly over to Dublin and launch a home-grow operation for him. But I made up an excuse about not being available because I didn't like the sound of what he was proposing. It was all to be done in an isolated farm, which is asking for trouble.'

Tig reckons you are far less likely to be caught with a home-grow operation in the city. He says: 'Best place of all is a loft in a terraced house. The police simply don't look for them in a city. But an isolated farmhouse in the middle of nowhere is an easy target for one of those helicopters with their infra-red cameras.'

Tig is referring to the much publicised but rarely used helicopters with special infra-red cameras used by UK police forces to check on such home-grow operations, which can be flagged up through their complex lighting systems.

But there are other risks involved in being a 'consultant', as Tig went on to explain: 'One time I helped this couple set up a home-grow operation in the loft of their house in Norfolk. Everything was going well until it got so hot in the loft that the weed literally started smoking. The smell was overpowering and you could whiff it from a hundred yards away. I tried everything to change things around to alter the temperature problem but the loft was south facing and the sun was turning it into an oven in the daytime. In the end, I had to abandon them.

'I warned them they'd get a pull very soon because their neighbours were sure to smell the weed. They ignored my advice and, surprise, surprise, the police paid them a visit, closed down the weed farm and they ended up getting eighteen months each for their troubles.

'You have to be careful. It's not quite as easy as people think. I guess that's why I have so many people queuing up for my services! The cultivation of the plants is essential and they need round-the-clock attention. Just chucking a few seeds in a plant pot is not going to get you anywhere.'

Tig's latest 'assignment' is to help a young aristocrat friend to set up a 'fucking huge operation' in one wing of his stately home. 'I've known this guy for years and we've smoked a lot of hash and weed together. But recently his dad died leaving him this fucking huge pile in Wiltshire but he can barely afford the local council taxes, let alone the rest of the running costs for the property.

'He asked me to take a look and see if I thought there was potential for a home-grow factory. Well, it was the dream scenario because there was a completely separate wing, which hadn't been touched in years. It was about the size of three terraced houses in square metres, so it had the potential to grow literally hundreds of plants.

'The only problem was my friend was so broke he couldn't afford to pay me a consultancy fee. I looked at the longer term and broke my own golden rule and agreed that he should pay me a 25 per cent mark-up on every plant that produced decent enough weed for him to sell on to a handler. I think it will turn out to be a very lucky move because once he gets going I will rake in a very healthy monthly retainer from his sale. I've also persuaded him to use the offcuts to produce hash as well, so it looks set to be the answer to all his financial problems.'

In some ways, Tig seems to see himself as some kind of Robin Hood depriving the rich, evil gangs of drug importers by encouraging everyone he knows to 'grow their own'. But of course there is a financial incentive from every person he helps, so it's not quite the charity he likes to make out it is.

'An old friend of mine recently told me I was like the saviour of the pot industry in this country. I like that description. It suits me down to the ground. I am a gentle old soul and all I really want is to make sure everyone is happy and rich!'

After our initial meeting in a pub in south London, Tig takes me to a nearby home-grow factory in the loft of a large semi-detached house in Lewisham. The owner greets Tig like a long lost old friend and he is equally polite to me. This is not anything like I had previously experienced inside the secret criminal underworld of hash.

We climb the staircase to a landing where a special attic ladder is sitting leaning against the wall. I can feel the heat wafting down from the loft immediately. Above me ultra-violet lights buzz lightly. We go up the ladder and find ourselves entering a netherworld of pot plants. They fill every inch of space apart from a narrow passageway through the middle of the loft area. It's baking hot. Almost like a sauna or a steam-room.

'The only problem with these sorts of operations is that they are a high fire risk,' explains Tig. I am not surprised. It feels as if one lit match would ignite and explode instantly.

Then Tig agrees to pose for a photo for my book on condition he disguises his face. 'I am immensely proud of this one. It's like my baby. I have nurtured this "grow" so carefully and now look at the result.'

It is certainly a stunning scenario. Dozens upon dozens of seeding cannabis plants reaching at least three foot in height make the attic feel more like a jungle than a suburban loft in a nondescript Victorian house. The smell is not so much overpowering as all-consuming.

As I descend the ladder I feel a bit dizzy from inhaling the air in the loft. Tig and I then head downstairs to the kitchen for a cup of coffee. Tig's openness, even in front of his 'client', is almost disarming. He treats the other man like a friend and persuades the man to pose for my camera with a disguise on.

'Yeah. I always tell people that the fire risk is very high on an operation like this. You have to be very careful. A couple of months back I helped set up one grow factory. Two weeks after I left some idiot lit a cigarette in the plant room and the house was turned into an inferno in minutes. Luckily the guy running it got out okay. I just hope the owners of the house [it turns out to have been rented] were insured because there wasn't much left of it.'

Naturally, Tig prefers to avoid any contact with the police. 'The police have their job to do and I have mine. One of the most important aspects of my consultancy business is to ensure that the factory is 100 per cent discreet. I explain to my clients that it's not just about growing plants. They have to be very careful whom they tell about their operation. They must never allow visitors to their house anywhere near the growing rooms and most important of all, they need to make sure their neighbours don't have a clue what is going on. The neighbours are the ones who most often end up informing the police.'

However, Tig says he is excited by the 'new challenges' he faces with his plans to encourage clients to make hash from their cannabis plants as well as grass. 'It makes such good economic sense. You can double your income virtually overnight by simply using the remains of each plant to make hash. I just can't work out why it was never done before.'

But, I point out, doesn't producing hash mean a completely different kind of customer? 'Good point,' agrees Tig. 'Most people either smoke weed or hash. The hash smokers here in the UK seem to be on average older than the grass users. Quite frankly, that's good news for me because most of my contacts and customers are middle-aged and I know I'd much rather be flogging hash to middle-class, middle-aged folk than walking into a squat with a bag of pungent weed.'

Back in that 'home-grow' house in Lewisham, owner Ronnie explains why he brought in the 'consultant' in the first place. 'Tig is a bloody genius. He helped me set this up from nothing, literally. He nurtures the plants as if they are his children. It's a very organic process and he is the key to its success.'

Ronnie admits that the 'grow' has been set up in the attic of his house for 'commercial and personal' reasons. He explains: 'I like a good smoke but I lost my job three months ago and, quite frankly, I am hoping that I can grow enough weed and produce enough hash to pay my way through life and get a good smoke thrown in for free!'

Ronnie says his wife knows all about the grow, but since the house itself is owned by his in-laws, he is keeping it a secret from everyone else he knows. 'Look, I know they'd be pretty angry if they knew what I was up to and I also don't want my mates knowing because they'd be round here all the time trying to get me to give them some free smoke. No way!'

Just then Tig gets a call on his mobile. He mutters a few brief words before clicking it off. 'I'm off to take my daughter to the zoo.'

And with that 'The Consultant' disappears back into the 'normal' world to take his child to a nearby zoo. I get the impression that Tig likes to stay in touch with that *other* side of his life.

CHAPTER 19

THE ALBANIANS' 'UK REP'

Foreigners – mainly eastern Europeans – are accused of more than one in four of all crimes committed in the UK. Astonishingly, they also make up nine out of ten drug suspects and are responsible for more than one in three sex offences. And according to one newspaper investigation Polish, Romanians and Lithuanians are the most likely of all foreigners to be prosecuted by the police.

The figures back up fears of an 'immigrant crime wave' and officials believe that it's not helped by the ease with which so many eastern Europeans are able to get into Britain with false identities, which hide their criminal past.

But nowhere illustrates this problem more than Albania. The collapse of law and order in that country has created a criminal element even feared by the Italian Mafia. I met Albanian hash baron Ivan in the UK through an introduction from a British gangster called Jerry, who warned me in advance that Ivan was 'a right fuckin' nutter'. One of Jerry's team of drug smugglers was stabbed in front of his eyes with a Samurai sword when another Albanian called Dimitri 'got upset' during a meeting in the Albanian port of Vlorë just a few months earlier.

Jerry explained to me: 'They are the maddest, baddest people I've ever met. Step out of line and they murder you – literally,' he says. 'The Albanians are the ones we all fear. They've got a stranglehold on virtually all the hash that comes in from east of Albania. You cross them at your peril.'

He's talking about hash smuggled from places such as India, Nepal, Afghanistan and the Lebanon. A lot of it is now primarily controlled by Albanians once it enters their country en route to the lucrative western European and US markets.

Jerry brought Ivan to a pub near Braintree, in Essex, to meet me. It's clear from the start of our meeting that Ivan is reluctant to talk and he's only there to keep his British friend Jerry happy. It's a bit like treading through treacle speaking with Ivan at first, despite his fine grasp of the English language.

Initially, he just sits and listens as I make harmless small talk with Jerry. Eventually I change tactics and ask Ivan out of the blue how he got into the hash 'game'. He says: 'I come from a long line of smugglers in Albania. In the village where I grew up that was the only way to make money. My family controlled everything that went in and out of the area. That's how we Albanians make our living. We charge people to bring their drugs through our territory. Why not?'

Jerry had already provided some of Ivan's backstory, so I knew that Ivan and his gang first began dealing in hash when a team of Turks tried to avoid paying them for the rights to pass through their area of Albania. 'We don't like Turks much, so we asked them for a lot of money for permission to come through our area. They sneered at us and tried to avoid paying.'

The clash with the Turks ended in a bloodbath. 'We drove the Turks out and stole their hash.' From that moment on, Ivan and his gang began 'taking over' all shipments that came through from the east. 'Ivan convinced other Turkish gangs that they should sell on the hash to him so he could then take control of it from the moment it got into Albania,' explained Jerry, who seemed remarkably unperturbed by the Albanian way of operating.

Ivan nodded his head slowly in tacit agreement with what Jerry was saying but he still seemed reluctant to talk directly with me.

I noticed that Ivan didn't drink alcohol. When I asked him why he said he was a Muslim. I didn't pursue that line of questioning because it was clear he did not want to talk about religion.

So I then asked him how often he came to the UK to 'do business'. Ivan's reply stunned me: 'Oh, I live here half the year. I use a different identity because I spent some time in prison in Albania and the British would not allow me in if I used my real name. I like the life here in England but I also like to be back in Albania sometimes to make sure my friends do their jobs properly.'

Ivan then proudly announced he had two girlfriends – or 'wives' as he called them – in the UK and two other wives back in Albania. 'It's perfect. Yes?' he smiled. 'Most men would like to have my life, I am sure.'

A few moments later, Ivan spotted an attractive woman at the bar and looked across intently in her direction. 'But then again there is always room in my life for another woman.'

I asked Ivan how he managed to hold onto that lucrative hash route from Albania to the UK. 'It's not easy but I have many friends in high places, so I can always get my shipments through without any problems.'

How can you just 'take over' a business that travels across numerous borders and checkpoints before it even gets to the UK? 'Oh, that is easy. As I say, we know the right people to pay to make sure the hash is delivered here without problems. It's a good system together and most of the time it works well.'

He turns to glance up at Jerry, who's just returned from the bar with some fresh drinks. 'Jerry is the only man in England I trust. He is a good man.'

Jerry throws in a smile for good measure.

Ten years ago, few people knew anything about Albania. Today, its gangsters have become so notorious for violence they are said to have even given the Italian Mafia a run for their money.

In the north of Italy, the Albanians are rumoured to have taken the prostitution racket away from the country's toughest

Mafia branch, the 'Ndrangheta. In the south, they control the drugs, guns, prostitution and human trafficking across the Adriatic and have forced an alliance with local Mafia groups. Even priests who work with women sold into sexual slavery must travel with bodyguards in case Albanian kidnappers take revenge.

UK investigators suspect the flood of hash into the country from the east is a direct result of Albanian criminals working under false identities in Britain.

Back in that Essex pub, Ivan knocks back his Coca-Cola and suggests we talk outside while he has a cigarette. It is bitterly cold but neither Jerry nor I is going to argue with Ivan.

In the pub garden, Ivan clearly feels it is safer to speak and he begins to explain in more detail about his gang. 'We are all related. We don't trust most outsiders. But no one fucks with us, eh Jerry?' He continues: 'We have the route from Albania to here airtight. Nothing gets in and out of my part of Albania without me knowing about it.'

'But why hash?' I ask.

'Because more people use hash than anything else, my friend. It's just another commodity to us. Hash. Coke. People. We will bring anything in if there is a demand for it. But hash is the biggest business, so we make sure we control it.'

Many of the British gangsters I have met down the years seemed to live in fear of Albanian mobsters like Ivan. 'They're animals, son,' one old-time south London drug baron told me. 'They shoot first and ask questions later. Horrible, cold people. They don't work to rules. If you upset them you're dead. Simple as that.'

So, how does the hash get in here? I ask.

Ivan's eyes narrow. He looks across at Jerry, then takes a long drag of his cigarette. 'I cannot tell you that then all the scum would try to steal my business.'

So I try a different tack. 'What happens when you lose a shipment of hash?'

'What d'you mean?'

'Is it the responsibility of those who are in charge of it?'

'Of course.'

'Do they have to pay you back its value?'

'Of course.'

'And what happens if they do not pay you back?'

'Then we don't use them any more.'

Albania's emergence as a chilling criminal 'power' has evolved since 1990. Following the collapse of the old Communist regime, 80,000 of them turned up in Italy within months. Albanian gangs quickly branched out from ferrying their countrymen across the Adriatic. Customs officers in Puglia, Italy, say every drug smuggler they catch is Albanian, often a refugee working off the cost of their US$500 passage.

Albanian criminal gangs have developed into sophisticated – and little understood – organisations profiting from globalisation. In the mid-1990s, the Albanian Mafia even brought over hash-growing experts from other countries to help introduce the crop to Albania. Ivan claims that about one-third of the hash he now handles is grown in Albania.

'But it's not as good as the stuff from further east,' he says. 'Most of the hash we produce in Albania goes to the Albanians because it is cheaper.'

Ivan is at pains to describe Jerry as his 'British partner' but it becomes increasingly clear as the conversation continues that Ivan is running a vast network of hash smugglers of which Jerry is a small part.

The Albanians who first turned up in Italy in the mid-1990s were used by the Mafia to do their dirty work, the jobs that had previously been done by people under eighteen who would not be sent to jail. The Albanians were willing to kill and they just didn't take life as seriously. They became the street dealers and the enforcers. 'The Italians were the brains and the Albanians became their hands,' said one expert.

I asked Ivan what would happen if the British authorities tracked him down in Albania and demanded his extradition. 'That will never happen because I have friends in the Albanian politics who can guarantee my safety. In any case, no one in England knows my real name!'

European police and lawmakers cannot mount an effective investigation into the criminal organisations based in Albania because the justice system there is barely functioning. The UK even refuses to have any agreements with Albania because reciprocity would require that UK citizens be exposed to the Albanian court system.

There are long, awkward silences as we sit in the bitter cold while Ivan chain-smokes and carefully thinks over the answers to each of my questions. Wearing jeans and a thick leather bomber jacket topped off with a skinhead haircut, he pervades coldness and evil. Other people in the pub seem to avoid any eye contact with him – and it is easy to see how he strikes fear into his British counterparts.

Ivan takes a long and deliberate pause while he drags on his cigarette. 'You know, my friend?' says Ivan. 'I do not consider myself to be a criminal. I am a businessman making money for my family. I did not make people take drugs. I am simply feeding a demand like any other business. You understand?'

I nodded and then Jerry blatantly tried to change the subject.

'What Ivan means, old son, is that if you stitch him up he'll come looking for you, eh?'

Ivan laughed and heartily slapped my leg. 'Jerry is so . . .' he paused. 'Dramatic.'

With that Ivan stood up, shook both our hands and strolled out of the pub garden towards the car park. It was only then I noticed a dark BMW 5 series with two men sitting in it. They must have been there all the time.

'I told you he wouldn't give much away,' said Jerry.

Half an hour later, Jerry the Essex-based 'hash trader', as he likes to be known, took me down to the seaside to show me how cannabis often reaches these shores. In among the brush oak stood a wildlife conservation area lying between the sea and the main road. It's a favourite drop-off point for hash smugglers, explains Jerry.

Empty packs of cigarettes lie scattered around piles of discarded clothes and shoes. Jerry emphasises that this is not one of Ivan's 'operations' but a drop-off point for other foreign smuggling gangs. 'See these clothes?' he says, poking a pair of women's blue underwear with his foot. 'There must have been a woman among them.' The females are usually forced into prostitution to pay for their journey from Albania.

The hash-smuggling refugees, who arrive at night or early in the morning, are usually picked up by cars and vans waiting nearby.

In the past, they've found bodies buried in the sand of these barren, deserted beaches, casualties of the smugglers' indifference to the lives of their clients as they often force them to swim ashore. I suspect Jerry has himself been involved in some of these 'pick-ups' but he talks in the third person to avoid any awkward questions.

The hash trade is a classic example of the drug industry's globalisation, with the Turkish Mafia often trading hash to the Albanians who then use their international connections to ship it to Europe and the UK.

It's also said that the Albanian Mafia likes to exert extra power and influence by blackmailing fellow Albanian migrants around the world. 'The Albanian Mafia has a huge capacity to expand itself. Many times decent Albanians are obliged to help the Albanian Mafia,' says one expert. 'If there are no other Albanian criminals in a country, they ask for help from law-abiding Albanians and put pressure on their relatives at home, who have little or no police protection.'

Jerry looks a bit uncomfortable as we get back into his four-by-four to leave the beach area. He turns to me nervously: 'For fuck's sake don't land me in the shit, will you? Those fuckin' Albanians will cut me head off if they think I've grassed them up.'

CHAPTER 20

TONY THE MASTER SMUGGLER

No book about the secret criminal underworld of hash would be complete without the extraordinary story of Tony, probably the most successful full-time hash smuggler in the UK after the legendary Howard Marks. Tony is the head of a team of smugglers, renowned in the British underworld. Now aged seventy-four, Tony first started organising lorry-loads of hash from India and Afghanistan in the early 1970s. His transport company is run as a legitimate business, which on the surface deals mainly in fruit imported from these countries. But hidden beneath each shipment are millions of pounds' worth of hash.

Tony is one of the most unlikely people you'll ever find in the hash trade. In his youth in south-east London and Kent in the late 1950s and throughout the 1960s, he was a member of a gang of professional bank robbers, who even teamed up with some members of the Great Train Robbery team just before they pulled off the so-called Crime of the Century in 1963. Tony was, naturally, the transport man when these blags were committed. That means he was waiting in the getaway car to drive the robbers at high speed away from the scene of their crime.

'It was a great time back then. Robbers like us were treated like pop stars and we had the lot – wine, women and song. But I knew it was a risky business, so I kept my eyes and ears out for something else, something more secure.

'I knew nothin' about drugs back then. In fact they were the devil's candy as far as me and my mates were concerned. We'd never touch an aspirin let alone a line of cocaine. We used to sneer at people who smoked pot and label them "stupid hippies" and stuff like that.'

But Tony says the turning point in his attitude towards drugs came when he served a short stretch in prison in the late 1960s. 'That's when I first came across the stuff. I even took a few uppers in jail to help pass the time away but I never really got really into them like a lot of other people I came across. I always preferred a pint with a whisky chaser and still do to this day.

'But what I did realise after being in prison was that drugs were about to explode onto the streets and soon everyone would be after them. I was an opportunist and I wanted a piece of that action, so not long after I got out I put together a proposition with another villain I knew and we arranged to buy a big load of hash from the Lebanon, which was infamous for its Lebanese Gold hash back then.

'The only problem was we had to get the stuff back from the Lebanon. We believed we were paying rock-bottom prices but we didn't fancy being ripped off by a bunch of dodgy smugglers who'd end up skimming most of our profit in "transport fees" and probably nick half the hash for good measure.

'So I looked into what usually got exported from Lebanon and it was oranges back then. Well, that clinched it. I'd send a lorry over to pick up some oranges and we'd hide the hash under them.'

Tony decided the only way to make this work properly was to create a legitimate transport company, which he officially registered and proudly had painted on the side of the Bedford truck he purchased specifically for the pick-up of hash.

'It went like a dream. Me and my mate headed off to Lebanon by road. It was a hairy old drive through some quite dangerous areas but we never had a sniff of trouble. We picked up the oranges and the hash in Beirut and sailed back through customs in Dover without a worry in the world. I knew then and there this was a much more lucrative business than blagging could ever be.'

But back then, many of Tony's fellow gangsters continued to disapprove of any dealing in drugs, so he was very careful not to let most of them know what he was up to. 'Most of my crew were so anti-drugs back then I genuinely feared one of them might grass me up to the law because they would have thought I was scum to smuggle drugs, even puff.'

Tony claims he was one of the first traditional London villains to 'convert' to hash smuggling. 'It was a daring move back then but the profit I made from that first ever hash deal made it *the* business for me. I was hooked. I'd struck gold. After all, it's so much easier and back then the chances of being caught were virtually nil.'

Within five years, Tony's company had grown to a dozen lorries and he was even managing to make a profit from the legitimate importation of fruit and vegetables, on top of his vast rake-offs from hash smuggling. 'It's funny 'cos none of my mates really cottoned on to what I was up to. They all just thought my legit transport business had hit the jackpot and that's the way I liked to keep it back then.'

Tony genuinely feared that one of the big criminal families who dominated the London crime scene in those days might try and muscle in on his business. 'I wasn't stupid and I knew there were people circling my company and trying to work out how I was doing so well. But I kept on smiling and making out the fruit and veg business was booming and most of them fell for it.'

Ironically, it was actually one of the last truly big heists that was to make things very complicated for Tony's business. 'In 1983, some of my oldest mates pulled off the Brink's-Mat robbery, which copped £27 million worth of gold. It was the biggest crime ever committed and the police went crazy trying to round up any known associates of the gang and of course I was one of their prime suspects, even though I'd been out of the blagging game for years.

'The cozzers presumed my transport company had been used to take some of the gold bullion abroad and raided my company just as a lorry returned from a run to Turkey. They found the stash of hash, I got nicked and had to close the whole operation down. I got five years for that little caper.'

Tony insists to this day he was innocent of handling any of the Brink's-Mat gold bullion but he accepted his jail sentence like a true pro. 'Listen. I may or may not have allowed one of my lorries to be used for some of the gold but at the end of the day, the coppers were after me for anything. They knew I'd been in the smuggling game for years and they were going to get me for something.'

When Tony emerged from prison three years later, he set up another transport company but this time he was even more savvy than before. 'I ran it entirely as a hundred per cent legitimate business importing and exporting fruit and veg. I did that for at least the first year after I got out of prison. It drove the coppers mad because they raided my premises three times during that period, convinced I was up to no good. But I knew I had to keep my nose clean for a while.'

Tony's hatred of the police was especially fuelled by that period. He explains: 'The coppers would harass me non-stop, sit on the gates to my house in cars and generally make a right pest of themselves. They enjoyed putting me through the wringer but I knew that when the time was right I'd set up another smuggling operation and they wouldn't even get a sniff of it.'

By 1990, Tony's police 'shadows' had pulled away from him after failing to arrest him for any more offences following his earlier release from prison. 'That was when I knew it was the perfect time to get back into the hash game. Within less than a year we were running as many shipments as before I'd been sent down. It was magic.'

These days, Tony admits he is finally slowing down and two years ago he sold off the main part of his transport business to another criminal, who subsequently got arrested and jailed for smuggling. 'It didn't surprise me. This bloke didn't have a clue how to run a successful smuggling operation and he got blown out of the water by the police when one of his drivers decided to grass him up. It would never have happened if I'd still been running the firm.'

Tony admits he still runs a 'small smuggling operation', which uses just two lorries. 'It suits me fine. I'm still making good money from hash, although the mark-up on the fruit and veg has crashed. God knows how anyone can make an honest buck these days. That's why I stick to villainy.'

Tony adds: 'In many ways I owe everything I have to hash. I don't think it's harmed anyone that much and I feel that smuggling it isn't really a crime like it would be if I shipped the white stuff.'

Tony is reluctant to talk about the specifics of his operation today, except to say: 'I keep it small and tight. That way there are no leaks. I'm not really sure why I'm still in this game, though. I should be enjoying a quiet and peaceful retirement but I like the buzz from what I do. My missus thinks I am mad and keeps nagging me to close the company but I can't bring myself to do that as yet.'

Tony reckons the biggest irony of all is that nearly all his old criminal cronies from south London are either dead or in prison. 'They sneered at me for getting involved in the hash game at the beginning and by the time most of them finally woke up to the money that could be made it was too late and the majority went into the coke business, which seemed to them to be the easy option. But coke's a different ballgame from hash. The stakes are higher and so are the risks, which is why so many of them either got topped or ended up being nicked for a long sentence.'

Tony adds: 'I'm an old man now in a much younger man's profession but I tell you, I know all the tricks of the trade and I'll probably just do a few more runs and then quit while I'm on top.'

Tony pauses for a moment of reflection: 'Or maybe not.'

PART FIVE

LAW ENFORCEMENT

Law enforcement agencies across the globe claim they spend upwards of one billion dollars each year in a bid to stamp out hash smuggling but to little avail.

The Strait of Gibraltar is crossed by at least 1,000 vessels every day of the year. As a result, it is virtually impossible to police, not helped by the dispute between Spain and the UK over ownership of the British colonial territory of the Rock of Gibraltar. Numerous hash boats slip between the various authorities who patrol the narrow strip of water. As one hash gangster told me: 'Sometimes I think God put the Strait there specially for us. It bridges North Africa and Europe perfectly, which is rather handy because Europe is the world's biggest single hash market.'

So while Spain and the UK continue bickering over ownership of the Rock of Gibraltar, the secret underworld of hash slips beneath the radar to exploit that 'weakness' to great effect.

Indeed smugglers appear to be the only winners when it comes to the ongoing feud between the UK and Spanish governments over ownership of the Rock of Gibraltar. In 2011, the Royal Navy and Gibraltar police were accused of piratical behaviour after clashing with Spanish police who had arrested drug smugglers in British territorial waters. A Guardia Civil officer was left with arm injuries after two boats collided when the Gibraltar forces tried to snatch Moroccan hash gangsters from a Spanish customs ship, which was surrounded by seven Royal Navy and police vessels, further stoking tensions between the two countries.

Reports in the Spanish media claimed the situation was 'five minutes away from a clash of incalculable consequences'. The Guardia Civil later issued a statement alleging that its members had been subjected to 'serious insults, harassment and threats' and claiming the Royal Navy and Gibraltar police had acted like 'pirates, as in other times in the past'.

Earlier, in September 2010, a Royal Navy patrol from Gibraltar arrived close to the Spanish shoreline in the coastal resort of La Linea while chasing a drug trafficker on a powerful jet-ski launch. Witnesses said the British vessel came close to the town's San Bernardo beach while following the trafficker, who was eventually arrested on Spanish soil by the Guardia Civil and local police. Spanish media reported that the arrested man was carrying several bags of hash. The Spanish pointed out shortly afterwards that the British patrol boat was not fired upon for entering Spanish territory, unlike whenever the Spanish had cause to enter the waters around the Rock of Gibraltar.

It seemed logical to begin my look at the law enforcement war against the hash barons by talking to Spain's hard-pressed Guardia Civil.

CHAPTER 21

GUARDIA CIVIL

The Guardia Civil has a long and chequered history in Spain since they were a paramilitary organisation until the death of dictator General Franco in 1975. But today they are responsible for busting drug gangs across the nation. Commissioned in 1844, the Guardia Civil was formed to maintain order in Spain's wild countryside where bandits and malcontents roamed threatening the monarchy and government. The state needed to stamp its mark of authority upon an anarchic situation and the GC fitted the bill perfectly.

Their fearsome reputation made them figures of hate and revulsion, especially in Spain's furthermost southern region of Andalucia, where many of the residents were of Jewish, Arab and Romano stock and the population was renowned for having scant respect for authority. During the first thirty or so years of the last century, the Guardia Civil cracked down on the 'bandoleros' who ruled the mountain passes.

Many battles took place during which the Guardia Civil used their so-called 'fast response' squads on horseback. The final bandolero was killed by the Guardia as recently as 1934.

During the Spanish Civil War (1936–9), the Guardia divided almost equally between the Nationalist forces and the Republicans; whether that was a tactical move to ensure success whoever won, or whether it reflected the specific location of the various Guardia *cuartels* (barrack blocks built in most main towns to control the area) when the war started, the Guardia fought on both sides. But after the war the Guardia became victor General Franco's strongarm force, maintaining strict control over all rural areas, where dissidents were more likely to spring up.

Even after the introduction of tourism in Spain in the late 1950s, Franco encouraged his Guardia Civil to continue to use an iron fist. In the thirty years from the end of the Second World War they were a force to be feared by anyone who opposed the state and the 'status quo'. Then after Franco's death, the Guardia Civil virtually disappeared from public view, only to return with responsibility for tracking drugs and terrorists, including ETA, the military wing of the Basque separatist movement which went on to kill dozens of Guardia Civil officers in their homes or in full view of the public. Today's Guardia Civil also carry out traffic controls, as well as having a special nationwide remit to deal with organised crime, including human trafficking into Spain from Africa.

One of the Guardia Civil's biggest anti-drug operations is run from the southern port of Algeciras, just opposite

Morocco. The Guardia use superfast powerboats that constantly patrol the Strait for any suspicious vessels. It's an incredibly busy sea-lane and police admit they cannot check out every suspect craft but in their operations room at the Guardia Civil's headquarters near Algeciras port, they maintain round-the-clock surveillance of the sea through radar and carefully positioned long-lens remote control cameras.

Watching the mass of tiny dots moving slowly across the green radar screens in the Guardia Civil's operations room sums up the huge scale of the problem and the difficulties of policing such a busy shipping lane. There are literally hundreds of vessels sailing between the Spanish mainland, Gibraltar and Morocco at any one time.

Specially trained Guardia Civil officers can tell most of the time what sort of vessels are out there by their shape on the radar screen. But the officers know that smugglers often use 'sleeper vessels' to test out the Guardia Civil monitoring system. One officer tells me: 'Often they'll send a craft out ahead in the hope that it will be spotted by our radar. Then a patrol boat goes out to intercept it while the boat with the actual drugs slips quietly past thanks to the diversion that has been created.'

The Guardia Civil admit they are fully stretched and barely able to cope with the sheer number of smuggling vessels and only expect to catch around 10 per cent of the smugglers crossing the Strait at any one time. It also becomes apparent during my day with the Guardia Civil that they don't always consider hash smugglers to be 'serious criminals' because cannabis is less harmful than Class A drugs such as cocaine and heroin.

'Sometimes we have to prioritise suspected cocaine and heroin smuggling more than hash,' explains one officer. 'That doesn't mean we don't come down hard on the hash smugglers but, let's face it, cocaine is a much more dangerous substance so it is more important to get the bad guys behind those gangs than the hash boys.'

Down in the actual port of Algeciras, the Guardia Civil also regularly uncover shipments of hash hidden in vehicles coming across from Morocco. 'We know all their tricks and it's a lot easier to catch them coming off a ferry than out there on the high seas,' says another officer. 'A lot of smugglers use a van or a car to bring the hash in and it's easy for our dogs to smell. Even when it has been carefully wrapped in clingfilm and smothered in hair conditioner to disguise the smell, it only takes one fingertip to have touched the car body for our dogs to pick up a scent.'

On the day I spent with the Guardia Civil at Algeciras port, their border patrol officers did precisely that when one of their sniffer dogs picked up the scent of hash on the bodywork of a Spanish-registered people carrier, after it arrived via a ferry from Tangier. Officers later revealed they only uncovered the haul because one of the smugglers had touched the wing of the car without gloves when the hash was being hidden in the vehicle. That alone gave the Guardia Civil probable cause and they immediately dismantled the vehicle in a drive-in garage next to the actual border crossing. Officers eventually uncovered more than €200,000 worth of hash hidden in tightly-packed slabs beneath the floor at the back of the people carrier. The vehicle had been driven by a Spanish man with his wife and small child.

Guardia Civil officers say it's 'pretty common' for entire families to come through the port carrying drugs. 'They think it makes them look less suspicious and to an extent they are right. But I never cease to be amazed how any mother could want to put her child at risk in that way,' explains an officer.

Less than two hundred metres away in a parking lot for lorries which have been stopped by the Guardia Civil, plain-clothes officers are searching underneath a huge Volvo articulated lorry which they suspect is carrying a large shipment of hash. It belongs to a long-haired Spanish trucker called 'Angel' who is standing in handcuffs thirty metres from his lorry. Officers refuse to confirm how they knew about the vehicle but it is presumed they must have had a tip-off.

One detective explains: 'We are well aware that smugglers sometimes give us details about hash coming through in the belief that if they "sacrifice" that shipment another much bigger one will slip through unnoticed. It's a ruthless business because the guy driving the lorry ends up in prison thanks to his so-called friends, who were happy to sacrifice him for a bigger load.'

A group of plain-clothes officers stand next to the huge artic. One of them kneels beside a wheel and begins grappling with something underneath the axle. He shouts and swears as he continues pulling and prodding the area. Suddenly he lets out a cheer. 'Si. Si. Si.' Bingo. They've just found what they were looking for.

As dozens of plastic-wrapped bricks of hash come tumbling out of the underside of the truck, the officers standing nearby congratulate each other. It's a bizarre sight as the mass of small hash bricks tumble out from underneath the lorry as if the vehicle is having a massive shit.

In all, it turns out there is hash worth more than a million euros under that one lorry. The detectives insist that proves they were not acting on a tactical tip-off. 'Why would they want to risk losing a million euros' worth of hash? No, this was somebody who had a grudge against the smugglers and he wanted revenge.'

As three plain-clothes officers carefully begin stacking the hash in neat lines alongside one of the tyres of the truck, my police guide takes a call on his mobile.

One of the Guardia Civil's green and white powerboats has just intercepted a boat on the other side of the harbour after radar monitoring officers noticed it steering erratically and very close to land. My police guide excitedly explained that as the Guardia Civil approached the boat, they saw three men on board pushing what looked like wooden crates overboard.

As the Guardia Civil powerboat closed in, the men dived into the murky water and swam for shore. Unable to get close enough to land on shore in the choppy waters, the

Guardia Civil on the powerboat radioed to colleagues to try and intercept the men as they watched them running across a nearby beach. Meanwhile the officers on the powerboat boarded the abandoned vessel to find it was empty, although they were convinced that the boxes being thrown overboard earlier must have contained drugs.

By the time we get the call to join them in another smaller Guardia Civil craft, two police divers are bringing up the boxes, which contain hundreds of carefully-wrapped slabs of hash. It's a surreal sight to watch the police divers keep coming up to the surface clutching more boxes.

But why would the smugglers try to offload the drugs so near to the Guardia Civil border control building, which was only about 500 metres from where their boat was spotted? One officer explains: 'They probably reckoned we wouldn't think they were suspicious because they were out in broad daylight and so near to our base. To be honest about it, if they hadn't stayed in one place for so long we probably wouldn't have bothered with them for that very same reason.'

We bob about on the choppy waters as more boxes are brought up by the police. Three Guardia Civil patrol cars appear on the strip of land opposite where we are. But the men have long gone. 'That's the other thing,' adds the officer. 'They knew they could make a run for it because they were so close to land. They probably even had a car parked somewhere nearby to escape in.'

The most astonishing thing about my day with the Guardia Civil is that in the space of what they insisted was 'just an ordinary day' they had uncovered three big shipments of hash.

I was impressed until one of the senior officers points out: 'Just think about it. We've managed to stop three shipments of hash but probably ten times that amount slipped past us today.'

Back at the quayside after the two Guardia Civil powerboats have docked, a group of officers offload the boxes of hash they've just recovered from the bottom of the sea. As the last box is piled on top of the others, Commandante Jorge Figuera steps forward proudly and invites me to watch as he pulls a huge hunting knife out from his belt and digs the point of it into a tightly packed brick of hash. With a small quantity of the brown substance on the tip of his knife he lifts it to his nose and inhales.

'Mmmmmmm. That is top grade hash. No doubt about it.' Figuera sounded more like a dealer than a policeman. 'What balls those guys must have to think they could smuggle all this hash right under our noses next to one of the busiest ports in the world. They are either *loco* [mad] or stupid. Maybe both!'

Just then, word comes through that the three men who swam ashore from that boat had, after all, been caught by Guardia Civil hiding in a nearby derelict warehouse. There is jubilation among the Guardia Civil officers, especially when they hear that the men surrendered without any resistance.

Half an hour later, Figuera invites me into the main building of the Guardia Civil next to the quay. As we walk through the office area I notice three scruffy men in damp clothes sitting in front of a desk having what looks like a friendly chat with a plain-clothes officer sitting opposite them.

Figuera proudly points out these are, indeed, the men who jumped off the hash boat and they are being 'interrogated' by a Guardia Civil detective. It looks more like an informal chat and two of the 'prisoners' are sitting there smoking. They all look extremely relaxed, even maybe relieved.

Figuera explains: 'Here in Spain we treat all prisoners with respect. I mean they are human beings like us. They most probably have families to support and, sure, they've got themselves mixed in crime but there are many in the Guardia Civil who feel that busting hash gangs is taking up much too much of our time. We should be concentrating on the big boys; the terrorists, the coke and heroin smugglers, the people smugglers.'

It seems that Figuera is trying to make a point about the 'seriousness' of hash smuggling and the criminals who carry it out. Figuera continues: 'Hash is everywhere here in Spain. It's smoked on the streets, in people's homes, even in shops and restaurants. Maybe it's time to legalise it and let us get on with catching the really evil gangsters and terrorists.'

As Figuera talks, I watch further interaction between the three hash-smuggling suspects and their so-called interrogator. Suddenly one of the men gets up and disappears through a door. No one even reacts to him leaving. Three or four minutes later the man returns having obviously been to the toilet.

I ask Figuera what he thinks will happen to the men caught with the boatload of hash. 'Oh, they'll probably either plead guilty if they are Spanish, serve a short sentence and then go back into the world of hash, I guess. Or if any of them are foreign, they'll probably be refused bail until they come up with a surety of at least fifteen thousand euros. Then they hand that over in exchange for their passports and no doubt they will leave the country within hours of their release.'

From my previous encounters with the Spanish authorities, I knew only too well that they believed it was cheaper for their judicial and prison system for foreigners suspected of drug crimes to pay a hefty surety before they are released on bail and then encouraged to immediately leave the country and never return. I know of three British drug smugglers who each had to pay €15,000 to get bail and then left the country.

One Guardia Civil officer admits: 'It saves Spain's courts and prisons so much money and we rid ourselves of them from this country for ever. It makes complete sense. Spain is in the middle of a huge recession. Why would we want to waste our money keeping foreigners in our prisoners and paying for them to have lawyers in court?'

CHAPTER 22

DETECTIVE MO

Moroccan police are notoriously slippery and their connections to drug-smuggling gangs have been well documented in the past. So it was with some trepidation and not a whole load of trust, I arranged to meet a recently retired Tangier detective called Mo in one of the port city's biggest cafes.

Hash gangsters and the police have close connections in these parts. It was similar to the way that in the 1970s, London's Flying Squad of elite detectives courted some of the capital's most notorious robbers and ended up in a sea of corruption and bribery that still reverberates in the UK's capital city to this day.

Mo the ex-detective turns out to be a very friendly character, who immediately admitted to me he'd been thrown out of the police force after being accused of accepting a bribe. He made it sound as normal as directing traffic. But Mo insisted he'd been framed by his colleagues after having an affair with his boss's wife.

'Things work very differently here in Morocco from London. The police are poorly paid. They have old equipment. Even the computers are fifteen or twenty years old and we never have any proper time to devote to solving crimes. If a murder occurs here in Tangier, our bosses give us a couple of days on the case and then insist we give up and move onto other stuff.'

I'd earlier heard from the two hash middlemen Leff and Fara that Mo had previously been stationed in Ketama, the notorious 'gateway' to the hash communities of the Rif Mountains. Mo shook his head as he recalled his time in Ketama. 'Ah yes, Ketama. That was not a good time for me because the hash gangsters did not like me being in their town.'

Mo believes he was sent to work in Ketama by a group of renegade detectives who wanted him 'out of the way' after he stumbled on a huge drugs racket inside the Tangier detectives' bureau. 'I guess they hoped I'd get killed by the drug barons,' he says with a wry smile.

He admits that during his three-month stay in Ketama, he was threatened 'many times' with death if he tried to stop any of the hash farms from operating in the mountains near by. 'I am a realist and if a hash gangster tells you to keep away from them in a place like Ketama you do as they ask, otherwise they slit your throat.'

Mo is convinced, like so many Moroccans I spoke to, that

Ketama and the surrounding Rif mountains will 'stay independent as long as it produces hash'. He explains: 'Hash is the lifeblood for the people in the Rif Mountains. When I turned up in Ketama they could have easily killed me, thrown my corpse into a valley and let the wolves feed on my carcass. But they are clever. They let me stay there but they made sure that anything I tried to do they would know about. If I called in a unit of police from Tangier they'd find out before I'd finished making the phone call. I had people following me around the town. They even put someone outside my rented apartment at night just to make sure I didn't try and slip away.

'I worked there with two hands tied behind my back. It's just the way it is there but I learned a lot about the Berber people. They are proud and secretive but they are also very clever and well organised. They know they have their own "kingdom" up there in the mountains and they want to keep it that way.'

Mo continues: 'I was considered a real high flyer in the force until I had some problems with the wife of my boss. I had the ear of the chief of police and I was often handpicked for difficult investigations but I guess I got overconfident. I thought I was invincible at work and with women. I pushed my luck too far but that doesn't make me a bad person or a bad cop.'

But what about the relationship between the hash criminals and the police? How close is it really? Mo hesitates for a few seconds while carefully considering his answer: 'There is no point in pretending that few of the police here in Morocco are corrupt. It's the only way many of them can make enough money to support their families. The bosses know what is going on but most of the time they turn a blind eye because they know how badly paid police officers on the ground are.

'The trouble is that everyone knows you can make a fortune from hash. No one, even the King himself, would ever do anything to endanger that business. It's vital to the economy. That's why the Berbers are left to run their own region. No one wants to do anything that will slow down the hash business because that would mean putting hundreds of thousands of people out of work. It would be a disaster for this country.'

Mo blames a lot of the problems connected to hash on foreign gangsters trying to set up their smuggling rings inside Morocco.

'Foreigners come here and try to take our income. We cannot allow it. They must understand and respect this country and not try to take things over.'

I recalled how Si, my British 'guide' in the Rif region, told me that at least half a dozen Dutch and Brits had been killed in recent years in the mountains after trying to set up their own hash supply chain directly into Europe.

'You need to understand just how powerful the hash gangsters are,' Mo said. 'They run the local government in the Ketama and the Rif region. They own all the big businesses and the locals know that without them they would be starving and destitute.'

He was starting to sound like some kind of public relations expert working on behalf of the hash barons.

'Sure, I know these guys. I've been to eat at their homes. I know what they are doing but as long as they remain the big employers in the area they will be untouchable. They are much more clever than the straight politicians. They know how to keep the people on their side.'

Mo's voice lowered as he told me of one gang of Spanish criminals who were attacked and killed by Berber hash barons when they turned up in Ketama ten years earlier. 'Everyone in Ketama talks about it. The Berber drug lords heard about the Spaniards within hours of their arrival. They sent a team round to the hostel where the Spaniards were staying and herded them into two trucks and drove them into the mountains. They were never seen again.'

As Mo the ex-cop spoke to me he became more and more animated and loud. It was only then I noticed that his nose was running and he seemed very edgy. When he went to the toilet for the third time in under an hour, I concluded that Mo was probably snorting cocaine.

As a result, the topics of conversation jumped around like a starling on heat. Suddenly out of nowhere, he begins talking about how he often smoked hash himself. 'Listen, there is nothing bad about hash. It helps people relax. I think a lot more people should smoke it then the world might be a happier place. When I was in the police, we used to all enjoy a joint or a pipe at the end of the day to unwind. Mind you, the hash we used was top grade because it had been confiscated from drug smugglers!'

Then Mo made a chilling revelation about my movements in Morocco. 'I know exactly where you have been throughout your trip here. The police were asked to keep an eye on you as they are with many writers or journalists. We Moroccans do not want negative things written about us.'

So, I asked, did he want hash to be made legal?

'Now that is a good question. I think it's better it stays like this because if big corporations got involved then a lot of those poor people up in the Rif Mountains would be out of work. Hash is engrained in their souls. It is part of their culture. Nobody in Ketama, for example, feels that hash is a criminal industry. It is looked on as being the lifeblood of the region.'

I then asked if Mo thought the King of Morocco himself was a hash smoker. He laughed. 'No way. He is too serious and careful to use hash but sometimes I think he'd be a lot more chilled out if he did smoke it.'

The most awkward moment of the interview came towards the end when Mo got quite agitated when I tried to change the subject after he unsubtly suggested I might pay him for the interview. I tried to ignore him but his coke-fuelled brain wouldn't let go that easily. I explained that the budget for my book didn't stretch to paying for interviews.

'You know, my friend,' said Mo, sounding much more tense than at any other time during our meeting. 'You people come here and try to insult our country and then you don't even appreciate that our time costs money.'

He said nothing more. Got up, nodded vaguely in my direction and left the cafe very quickly.

It was lucky he left that golden question until the end because I have no doubt he would have walked out much earlier if he knew I didn't have a bribe to pay him.

CHAPTER 23

UK LAW ENFORCEMENT

Britain's Royal Navy comes into contact with so many smugglers during patrols of the Strait of Gibraltar that they have dubbed this strip of water the 'Hashish Highway' because they reckon that 70 per cent of the world's hash travels across these waters each year. The navy spends more time boarding suspected drug smugglers' boats than protecting the waters around Gibraltar from maritime intruders. Stopping drugs reaching British shores – or any shores for that matter – has become a key mission for the Royal Navy and its subsidiaries the Royal Fleet Auxiliary and Fleet Air Arm in recent years.

At any one time, a navy destroyer and frigate are stationed in Gibraltar from where regular patrols of the North Atlantic are carried out, as well as numerous stop and search operations in the British waters off the Rock. Hash traffickers in the area are renowned for often using what are known in the drugs trade as 'go fasts' – inflatable speedboats packed with petrol and drugs – to try and outrun the authorities.

The Gibraltar government's own Police Marine Section (RGPMS) also patrol the same waters in co-ordination with the Royal Navy. They operate two purpose-built patrol boats, considered crucial for patrolling the shallower waters close to the Rock. These new smaller vessels play a key role in combating crime and drug trafficking in Gibraltar waters.

One of the RGPMS vessels is an all-weather interceptor powered by four outboard engines and fitted with a fully enclosed cabin. The second boat does not have an enclosed cockpit but a hard canopy to protect the crew from the elements. Both 13-metre vessels are equipped with numerous safety features – including hydraulic suspension on crew seats – and are capable of navigating at high speed in rough seas.

But the RN and Gibraltarians are incredibly sensitive to stories about the Rock's connection to drugs and crime. One Gibraltarian vet explains: 'The Rock is still a hotbed for dodgy criminals and drug smugglers but the Gib government doesn't want to encourage anyone to say that in public so they play down the drug smuggling.'

So I turned to the UK mainland for the real story about how Britain is taking on the secret world of hash.

In Britain it is the job of the UK Border Agency (UKBA) to try and stem the tide of hash coming into the country. The agency was formed on 1 April 2008 by a merger of Britain's Border and Immigration Agency (BIA), UK Visas and the

Detection functions of HM Revenue and Customs. The decision to create a single border control organisation was taken in a bid to tighten Britain's borders to prevent smuggled goods, such as drugs – including hash – from entering the country.

The UK Border Agency's staff of 23,000 people is located in over 130 countries. Overseas staff vet visa applications and operate an intelligence and liaison network, acting as the first layer of border control for the UK. But the agency's main role is to investigate all aspects of drug smuggling by developing a single primary border control line at the UK border monitoring all people and goods entering the country. With a budget of £2.2 billion the UK Border Agency certainly has the funds available to be an effective force in the battle against hash smugglers.

But most of the British hash gangsters I have spoken to for this book claimed that despite their public pledges to the contrary, the agency has done little to stem the flow of hash into the UK, although the UKBC would no doubt disagree and they have certainly been trying to publicise their so-called 'crackdown' on hash in recent years.

Unlike their Spanish counterparts the Guardia Civil, the UK Border Control (UKBC) were extremely reluctant to help me with my research for this project. It was frustrating because the UKBC's efforts to catch hash smugglers had led to a number of very dramatic high-profile arrests in recent years and I wanted to hear directly from the men and women who claimed they were cracking down on the hash smugglers, as well as those dealing in more dangerous Class A substances.

Eventually I traced an old contact who'd been one of the top officials in the drugs investigation arm of the UK Customs and Excise before it was absorbed into UK Border Control. Part of his job had been to travel the world uncovering hash supply routes from places as far afield as Afghanistan and Tibet. He turned out to be a mine of information. We shall call him 'Robert' here to protect his identity since he still works undercover on a freelance basis for the UKBC and a number of other forces around the world.

Robert explains: 'There has been this tendency in recent years for nations to pull back from cracking down on hash in favour of concentrating on heavier drugs but in the UK we always believed that hash was an inevitable precursor to those more serious drugs and their associated addictions. Hash may not be as harmful in itself but the profits for smuggling it for the criminals are vast and I believe that many of those same smugglers also carry A-class narcotics.'

Robert continues: 'I know it may sound a tad old fashioned, but we believed and still do as far as I am aware, that hash is definitely worth our attention. It's helping feed a huge section of the underworld and it needs to be dealt with seriously and efficiently. Our partners in Europe and beyond are, quite frankly, useless. They are just not prepared to prioritise it. There have been many times when I've tried to discuss this with our alleged partners in the fight against drugs and realised everything I was saying was falling on deaf ears.'

He says that in his day dealing with the authorities in many of the Narco States such as Afghanistan, Morocco and Mexico was a 'nightmare'. 'I'd fly out to these place with appointments to see police chiefs and they wouldn't even turn up for meetings. I knew a lot of them were corrupt but you'd think they would at least go through the motions, surely?'

One time Robert tracked a major UK criminal's articulated lorry when it travelled across Europe into Turkey, where it picked up a shipment of hash, which had originally come from Afghanistan. Robert says: 'The idea was to make sure all the hash was on board and then track the lorry as it travelled back through Europe until it turned up at Dover. Trouble was that most of the countries it was going to travel through were riddled with corrupt police, so we decided we couldn't even inform them of our plans in case the cannabis smugglers got wind of what was happening. We just crossed our fingers and hoped the lorry would get to the UK eventually.'

Robert says that for the following ten days, his team continued shadowing the truck and then raided the vehicle within minutes of it driving off a ferry ramp in Dover.

'But it could easily have ended in disaster and I hated the attitude of all those different countries. No wonder criminals think that hash smuggling is a "safe" option compared with dealing in cocaine.'

Robert currently works for various countries as a consultant in drug prevention and anti-smuggling operations. 'It's been an incredible eye opener for me. So few countries even have a clear anti-drug policy. Most of them just don't have the finances to properly try and crack down on drug shipments. I often get hired to help on the ground officers learn how to uncover drug shipments but of course that is only a small part of the preventative programme. You need money and technical resources to really make a dent in drug trafficking.'

Robert is not optimistic about the future. 'I think the influx of foreign gangs into countries like the UK, France, Spain and Italy is already causing a flood of poor quality recreational drugs into those nations. These gangsters are desperate to make the biggest profits possible while they attempt to make a mark for themselves as criminals. Countries like the UK are being swamped with four times the amount of hash that used to come in as these criminals try to create huge markets out of substandard, dangerously-cut drugs, and that includes hash.'

And, says Robert, the authorities have little or no chance of infiltrating these gangs. He explains: 'The police and other authorities rely on informants but it's getting harder and harder to infiltrate these criminal gangs because they are such tightly knit groups. Informers are few and far between these days. The gangs from eastern Europe are so ruthless that other criminals don't dare cross them.'

Three years ago, Robert was given a six-month contract to work with the Afghan police to try and stem the flow of hash from the troubled, war-torn nation. 'It was pretty pointless. I felt as if I had been hired by the Afghan government simply to keep the Americans happy. None of the locals care about the illegalities of hash or even heroin for that matter. Many of the farmers have been selling it to the west for thirty, even forty years. They consider it a crop just like anything else and most of the local police feel exactly the same way.'

Robert believes that the Afghan government tacitly allows the cultivation of cannabis because it employs tens of thousands of Afghans. 'It's similar to Morocco but on a smaller scale,' he explains. 'I tried my hardest to explain the attitudes [to drugs] in the West to the Afghan police but even the top officials looked at me like I was mad.'

But it wasn't until Robert agreed to go for dinner at the house of a local police chief that he fully appreciated just how different that attitude was. He continued: 'It was typical Afghan generosity. This police chief laid on a huge meal for me with his family and friends in his house. I felt quite humbled when I turned up there and saw how much effort they'd made.'

Then two of the police chief's adult sons sat down either side of Robert. 'And d'you know what they did? They each lit up a hash joint and started smoking it there right in front of my eyes. I didn't know what to say, so I ignored it but then the police chief himself pointed out what they were doing and I realised it was a deliberate attempt to try and convince me that hash was part of normal Afghan society.'

Robert sums up: 'I don't know how we in the West can overcome those sort of attitudes towards hashish. Sometimes even I believe that it might be a whole lot easier if recreational drugs were legalised and then we could at least control it more closely but I can't see the politicians doing that in my lifetime, although they will in the end.'

PART SIX

HASH – ON A GLOBAL SCALE

If the current rate of new hash recruits continues it is estimated there will be one billion smokers by the end of this century.

PART SIX

HASH – ON A GLOBAL SCALE

CHAPTER 24

A WORLDWIDE SURVEY OF THE HASH BUSINESS

AFGHANISTAN

A recent United Nations report on cannabis in Afghanistan revealed that between 10,000 and 24,000 hectares of cannabis plants are grown in Afghanistan every year. While other countries have far larger cannabis cultivation, the astonishing yield of the Afghan cannabis crop (145 kilograms per hectare of hashish, the resin produced from cannabis, as compared to around 40 kg/ha in Morocco) makes Afghanistan the producer of the world's most powerful hash. The UN survey exposed large-scale cannabis plant cultivation in half of Afghanistan's provinces, where it is three times cheaper to cultivate a hectare of cannabis plant than a hectare of opium poppies. The UN has urged authorities to find legal crops for the Afghan farmers to make their income from, but there is little hope of this ever happening as long as worldwide demand for hash continues. And like so many terrorist groups across the globe, the Taliban's struggle against the Coalition forces is said to be subsidised by hash production.

ARGENTINA

In Argentina hash is an immensely popular recreational drug. In early 2012, the Argentine Navy stopped a lorry driver on an isolated coastal road in the province of Missiones after the vehicle was seen making a beachside 'pick-up' that turned out to be of more than a ton of hash. The navy also discovered an abandoned boat nearby. The final haul consisted of 822 bricks of hash with a weight of 1,047.49 kilograms, said to be worth at least $1 million on the open market.

AUSTRALIA

Australia's vast coastline is virtually impossible to police so authorities have fought a long and difficult war against hash smugglers. One of their few successes was in June 2012, when New South Wales police arrested 18 people and seized more than 20 kilograms of hash during simultaneous raids targeting the drug trade. Nearly 150 officers executed 18 search warrants at locations from the Sydney suburbs of Bondi and Cabramatta north to Tuggerah Lakes, Forster and Tamworth in a massive swoop by officers.

BALI

Bali fiercely protects its reputation as a safe, peaceful holiday island by warning hash users and smugglers they risk a death sentence if caught. Two Russian nationals are the latest narco-tourists to face the death penalty if convicted. One of them, a 30-year-old yoga teacher was held in Bali after arriving from the Malaysian capital, Kuala Lumpur with 88 hashish capsules in his stomach. Two days later another Russian national, a 43-year-old art designer swallowed 359 hashish capsules and was also arrested in the Bali airport. Both men had bought their hash in India and officials said the total value of the drugs was estimated at 966 million rupiah ($105,300). Meanwhile in neighbouring Indonesia, a 57-year-old Dutchman was arrested at Lombok's airport in 2012 after arriving from Singapore carrying 3.7 kilograms of hash in the lining of his suitcase. He also could face the death penalty if found guilty.

BRAZIL

In one notorious Rio *favela* (shantytown) called Mandela, drug dealers have stopped selling crack and encouraged more dealing in hash because they believe it is 'less harmful' to the community. The drug bosses, often born and raised in the very slums they now lord over, say crack destabilises their communities, making it harder to control areas long abandoned by the government. Law enforcement and city authorities, however, take credit for the change, arguing that drug gangs are only trying to create a distraction and persuade police to call off an offensive to take back the slums.

CANADA

Canada's role inside the secret underworld of hash is pivotal as it provides a gateway to the lucrative US market. As a result, there has been a steady increase in hash seizures over the last ten years. The home market for smoking has also increased significantly and latest Canadian statistics show the highest proportion of hash smokers in the country are aged between 15 and 24. Canadian authorities say that by targeting young people, traffickers are leaving a trail of ruined lives, unrealised potential, health care costs, lost productivity, crime associated with drugs and related violence which often affects a user's family and friends. In Montreal, the alleged head of a street gang of hash dealers was one of three men killed in the city during one deadly 48-hour period in early 2012. In Toronto, a much-feared hash gangster was deemed too dangerous to be released from prison after it was discovered he'd managed from inside jail to arrange hash shipments from Jamaica, tamper with a witness testifying against him and orchestrate an attack on an inmate at another prison.

CHILE

In October 2012, Chile proposed a bill that would legalise the consumption, possession and cultivation of marijuana. Prior to the introduction of the legalisation bill, one of its proponents even publicly admitted his own use of hash in an attempt to show that use doesn't equal abuse. But his comments prompted an attack by hysterical conservative opponents, who then spearheaded a bill to 'prohibit marijuana use in Congress'.

CHINA

China has a steadily increasing number of cannabis smokers. The Chinese government estimates that there are between 2 and 3 million drug users in China and at least one million of them smoke hash. To put these figures into perspective, when Mao came to power in 1949 there were an estimated 20 million drug users in China. Using harsh methods, including executions, the Communists were able to rid China of its drug problem almost overnight. Then in the 1980s, China opened up more and eased its border controls and drugs began flowing into the country. But it wasn't until the turn of the new century that drug use really took off. China still has tough, some would say draconian, drug laws. Getting caught dealing or trafficking even small amounts of hash can result in a death sentence. Meanwhile secret hash 'farms' have been set up in some of the poorer regions of the country. It is reckoned that over the next 20 years, the Chinese underworld will push up production in order to cash in on the international hash market.

COLOMBIA

Back in the late 1970s, Colombia was one of the world's major marijuana producers before it became better known for its cocaine production. Now drug barons are encouraging a comeback to their former days of hash glory. In the summer of 2012, Colombian police seized almost 10,000 pounds – nearly five tons – of marijuana with an 'estimated street value' of $5.5 million over the span of three days in the cities of Medellin and Pereira.

The city of Medellin – once notorious for its cocaine traffickers and birthplace of the legendary drug baron Pablo Escobar – is emerging as the new 'capital' for hash production. Police uncovered 5,000 pounds of cannabis in a truck carrying oranges in 2011. The massive payload – consisting of more than 101 bales of marijuana – weighed almost 6,000 pounds. That shipment belonged to a crime lord known only as

'Sebastian', head of the 'Oficina de Envigado', a crime syndicate founded by Pablo Escobar, which still allegedly holds majority control of Medellin's underworld.

DENMARK

In Denmark, Hell's Angels gangs dominate the hash business. In 2012, one such gang admitted smuggling 3.6 tons of hash. A court heard that the Danish police's gang unit, Task Force East, had gathered video surveillance of four bikers storing the drugs at various locations. The 53-year-old leader of the gang owned a sports car, jewellery, a large amount of cash and a villa – assets which he had earlier claimed came from a large lottery win. Near Copenhagen, a small 'hash' community has sprung up in a quiet village called Christiania. Visitors to the village are able to buy all grades of hash openly. Huge blocks of hash are openly displayed on tables on both sides of the main street on market stalls made of wood and plastic. Prices vary from €8 to €20 depending on the quality, claim the dealers. However, Christiania is much more than just a hash market. Inhabitants run it as a self-sufficient village with its own houses, a school and even a bar. One recent visitor described the village as 'a hash resort'.

GERMANY

The hash market in Germany is described by experts as 'steady' and 'very open' as authorities tend to take a lenient attitude towards smokers. Like Denmark, many of the hash gangs come from within the Hell's Angel biking communities. In 2012, police raided a Hell's Angels hide-out in the German city of Düsseldorf and entered a World War II bunker to find a huge cannabis plantation – complete with a round-the-clock team of professional gardeners.

GHANA

Hash barons have turned Ghana into a worldwide drugs hub. Often shipments of the drug from Morocco travel south to Ghana and Gambia before being flown or shipped back north into Europe. One hash baron was arrested in Gambia and then escaped police custody and took refuge in Ghana. He was eventually extradited back to Gambia in early 2012.

Investigations conducted by security agencies revealed that the same drug baron had travelled widely across the world, visiting countries such as the UK, France, Belgium, Benin, Bulgaria, Romania, Slovakia, Ecuador, Colombia, Venezuela, Jamaica, the UAE, Sierra Leone, Togo, The Gambia, Senegal, Mali, Cote d'Ivoire and Liberia.

GREECE

Hash production is rife on the holiday island of Crete. In many remote mountain villages, cannabis growers and dealers routinely take pot-shots at police helicopters or vehicles patrolling their area, prompting the Greek media to refer to this region as a 'Greek Colombia' and a 'narco state within a state'.

In 2010, three Greek police officers taking part in a raid on a hash plantation were ambushed and shot at by suspected growers armed with AK-47s. The attack took place in the village of Malades, about nine miles from Heraklion, the island's largest city. The shooting was the second serious attack by hash growers against police on the island in seven months. The Greek government responded with a massive police sweep and house-to-house searches. Police arrested 16 people in connection with the ambush and a series of bank robberies, but recovered none of the hash and very few of the heavy weapons, believed to have been used in that assault.

GUATEMALA

Hash is big business in Guatemala. Not only is it an ideal dropping-off point for drugs travelling to North America, but a large section of the local population smoke cannabis.

HASH

Crime cartels – many of whom smuggle hash – are said to be winning the multi-billion-dollar drugs war. The Guatemala government admits there is little hope of bringing most of them to justice. President Otto Perez Molina – who has spent more than 20 years on the frontline battling some of the most vicious drugs gangs in the world – says narcotics of all kinds should now be viewed in the same way as alcohol and tobacco – and legalised. Many of those fighting the powerful drug cartels in Central and South America agree with the Guatemalan president that legalisation of hard drugs is the lesser of two evils.

INDIA

Authorities in India are increasingly concerned by the criminal connections between hash production and terrorism. This was highlighted by the 2012 arrest of two men who worked for one of the country's most notorious hash barons, also suspected of being the mastermind behind the 1993 Bombay (now Mumbai) bombings that left over 250 dead. India claims that narco-terrorism is a threat to itself and the global community.

The US state department even published evidence that exposed the same Indian gangs' regular hash smuggling routes, which crossed South Asia, the Middle East, and Africa – from Afghanistan and Thailand to the US, western Europe, the Middle East, Latin America, and Africa.

HASH ON A GLOBAL SCALE

ISRAEL

There is a big hash-smoking culture in Israel, which is often overshadowed by the conflicts that continue to rage in that part of the world. In the capital Tel-Aviv, local cops don't even bother going after hash users and suppliers. Much of the hash consumed comes in via neighbouring Arabs. They smuggle it in through the West Bank, some of it wrapped in large bundles with eagles emblazoned on the seals, with the slogan, written in Arabic, 'We are the victors!'

ITALY

There is an ever-increasing demand for hash in Italy, thanks to millions of regular smokers. In July 2012, police in the south of the country arrested ten people and impounded over seven tons of hash in an operation against an alleged trafficking gang importing the drugs from Spain. The suspects were arrested and charged with drug trafficking. Police also recently seized seven tons of cannabis in the northern city of Genoa, during an operation that led to the international arrests of nine men in Canada and two in Pakistan.

JAMAICA

Hash has been a way of life for many growers and users here for many decades but in recent years the authorities have tried to 'clean up' the island's image by cracking down on the mass hash production on their doorstep. It's claimed that much of the confiscated hash eventually finds its way back onto the island's lucrative drugs market. But Jamaican authorities have now begun a programme of publicly destroying huge quantities of hash oil during burning operations on wasteland near the capital, Kingston.

JAPAN

Japan's notorious gangsters, the Yakuza, have been involved in the hash trade for centuries. This Japanese version of the mafia claims to be descended from Robin Hood-like characters, who defended their villages against roving bandits many centuries ago. But today, the Yakuza is a mighty and entrenched criminal network with nearly 80,000 members operating in 22 crime syndicates, and raking in billions of dollars a year, much of it from the sale of hash on Japan's streets.

KUWAIT

The emergence of hash in Kuwait has alarmed officials in the oil-rich kingdom. Two Kuwaitis were recently arrested for possessing hashish when their car was stopped for driving too close to the US Embassy in Kuwait City. Not long after this, a Kuwaiti youth was arrested by a police patrol for possessing hashish and was immediately handed over to the General Department for Drug Control.

In June 2012, a gang of hash smugglers dumped 242 kilograms of cannabis in the ocean off Kuwait when they spotted a Coast Guard boat approaching. Authorities had been alerted thanks to the Coast Guard surveillance system that detected a motorboat entering the territorial waters of Kuwait. The men on the boat threw two bags into the sea before they were arrested. A team of divers later retrieved the two bags.

LEBANON

Despite constant political turmoil in its capital Beirut, overstretched security forces and a lifeless economy, the farmers in the notorious hash fields of the Bekaa Valley have cultivated relatively large hash harvests since the 1980s. Lebanese police estimate that there are 16,000 acres of hashish in the Bekaa's sun-baked plain. In recent years,

Lebanese army units have tried to destroy the Bekaa hash crop as part of a Government-sponsored eradication programme. But it usually ends in chaos and bloodshed with angry local farmers and hash dealers turning their weapons on the troops because the farmers believe they have the right to grow cannabis. In Lebanon, hash is suspected of helping subsidise the Hezbollah terrorist group, accused of murdering Americans, Israelis, Lebanese, Europeans, and the citizens of many other nations. Originally founded in 1982, this Lebanese group has evolved from a local menace into a global terrorist network.

MEXICO

US drug enforcement officials believe that Mexico's most violent hash cartel, the Sinaloa, is trying to set up operations in Britain, France and the Netherlands. Three members of Britain's Serious Organised Crime Agency (SOCA) met US agents on the Texas-Mexico border in 2012 in a bid to put a stop to the Sinaloa taking hold in Britain and Europe. Mexican crime groups have previously made attempts to establish a presence in Europe but it seems that the Sinaloa is intent on pushing for worldwide 'rights' to the global hash market.

NEPAL

Nepal is renowned among hash smokers as the home of the finest hand-pressed hash on the globe. As a result, there is a relatively small but highly lucrative hash trade between Nepal and Europe, in particular. Yet some of the methods used by hash smugglers in Nepal down the years have defied belief. In the capital Kathmandu, in 2012, police found hash packed in tablet form in a consignment of ginger in a suitcase on a bus recently arrived from the city of Dhading. The smuggler had posed as a vegetable farmer but was caught by law enforcement officials after a tip-off.

Criminals have even turned their own houses into hashish factories. The hash is then smuggled to international cartels via India. One notorious gang shipped hash via Goa in India, wrapped in blankets that would ultimately land in different countries including the USA, UK, Canada, Japan and Germany. Officials believe much of the nation's cannabis also goes to China through a specially organised criminal network.

NEW ZEALAND

New Zealand is believed to have more hash smokers per head of population than anywhere else in the world. This means there is a big market for hash and the authorities are struggling to crack down on the hash gangs. A rare breakthrough in the battle against the drug barons came in July 2012, when property valued at more than $2 million in cities including Dunedin, Queenstown and Invercargill were linked to a multi-million-dollar cannabis-growing ring uncovered by police. The highly organised gang had been operating for decades in New Zealand and hash valued at $4.5 million was seized during the execution of search warrants by police.

PORTUGAL

In 2001, Portugal became the first European nation to decriminalise possession of all drugs – from marijuana to heroin – within its borders. While many critics feared the drug policy change would lead to drug tourism while simultaneously worsening the country's high rate of hard drug use, it is claimed that it did nothing of the sort.

RUSSIA

It is not clear how much, if any hash, is produced inside Russia but recent surveys suggest that millions of Russians now smoke hash on a daily basis. As a result of this demand, the notoriously cold-blooded Russian Mafia have spread their illicit tentacles into India, according to crime experts. Russian hash barons have homed in on an area around the popular

Indian coastal resort of Goa, India, where they have 'taken over' a number of local hash farms, as well as setting up secret supply routes back to the former Soviet Union.

SCOTLAND

In Scotland south-east Asian trafficking gangs are said to be the force behind its hash farm trade – with £40 million of the drug seized by cops in 2011 alone. The invasion of these eastern drug lords – who harvest cannabis in homes across the country – was first uncovered thanks to a local newspaper investigation.

In just over four years, police battling the immigrant drug gangs have seized enough plants to cover the three pitches at Glasgow football stadiums Ibrox, Parkhead and Hampden. Police believe the properties had been converted into drug farms by trafficked workers to rake in a fortune from the illegal trade. Of 304 people arrested three-quarters were Chinese, and 22 per cent were from Vietnam, mostly victims of the evil drug barons.

SINGAPORE

Singapore's draconian Misuse of Drugs Act punishes possession of even minuscule amounts of hash, and prescribes execution if you're found guilty of carrying large amounts of any drug.

Under the Misuse of Drugs Act, the burden of proof lies with the defendant, not on the government. If you're caught with large amounts of drugs, you are simply presumed by law to be trafficking. It goes even further: if you own a house or a car in which illegal drugs have been found, you are presumed under the law to have possession of the drug, unless you can prove otherwise.

SOUTH AFRICA

Well-organised gangs are said to be taking advantage of the rock-bottom price of South African hash – known locally as dagga – to enjoy profit margins as high as 4,000 per cent. Police are warning that those behind the trade could become richer and more powerful than those trafficking cocaine and heroin. Hash from South Africa and neighbouring countries is some of the most potent in the world and now accounts for a relatively large number of seizures in the UK.

SRI LANKA

The sunshine paradise island Sri Lanka – desperately trying to promote peace and stability after a generation of civil war – has stepped up its pursuit of hash criminals. In April 2012, police arrested a 23-year-old British national linked to a hash smuggling ring. The country's Police Narcotics Bureau (PNB) at the island's Katunayake airport detained the man as he attempted to leave for Thailand. He was a member of a street drama troupe and allegedly a drug addict. His friend, another British national, was arrested when he attempted to pick up the parcel left by the first man, which contained hashish hidden inside magazines. Both men deny the charges that have been levelled against them.

THAILAND

Two Chinese tourists visiting Thailand in 2011 were caught in possession of hash in the town of Naklua. They claimed they were unaware that hash was illegal in Thailand. The police did not accept their excuse for smoking and possessing the drug and the pair were locked up to await a court appearance.

TURKEY

A total of 26 tons of cannabis were seized in a police anti-trafficking operation in the province of Diyarbakir in south-eastern Turkey, in July 2012. Local officials claimed the hash had been produced by the banned Kurdish Workers' Party (PKK) and the Kurdistan Communities Union (KCK), an umbrella political organisation that includes the notorious terrorist group the PKK. In the towns of Lice, Hazro and

Kocakoy in Diyarbakir, the PKK and KCK openly grow cannabis and turn the majority of it into hash. The PKK is labelled as a terrorist organisation by the European Union and the United States, and it seems drug trafficking is a main source of its income.

UAE

In January 2011, police in the city of Sharjah made their biggest drug haul in 20 years after seizing 2,534 kilograms of hash at a local port following a tip-off and sting operation. The drugs were found in a ship transiting through Khorfakhan waters. Police said they were tipped off when the smugglers began searching for a local buyer for their hash.

Police eventually arrested twelve Iranians and two Pakistanis in connection with the bust. The boat was brought to shore by a tugboat, and the suspects confessed to planning to smuggle the drugs into the UAE.

UNITED STATES

The US continues to pile pressure on many hash-producing countries to eradicate all cannabis harvesting, and the world's most powerful nation regularly passes some of the heaviest sentences in the world for those connected to the hash business. The Oklahoma Senate recently passed a bill that would mandate a sentence of up to life in prison for making hashish out of marijuana.

VIETNAM

Vietnam became renowned for its high-quality hash during its 10-year war with the United States, but the communist government in power since the war ended in 1975 has some of the toughest drug trafficking laws in the world. Despite this, buying pot in Hanoi is 'very easy', and it costs about 100,000 VND – about $6 – a joint.

In 2009 five Chinese men, ranging in ages from 42 to 57, were sentenced to death in northern Vietnam for trafficking almost eight tons of hash destined for Canada. The cannabis came from Pakistan and was about to be shipped to North America through the Vietnamese port of Mong Cai when Vietnamese customs agents swooped.

APPENDIX

THE DIRTY DOZEN
BIGGEST EVER HASH BUSTS

- Afghan police in the province of Kandahar seized what is reckoned to be the biggest stockpile of hash ever recovered, in 2008, with a wholesale value of $400 million. The hash weighed 261 tonnes – as much as 30 double-decker London buses – and was found hidden in several trenches. The region is about 40 kilometres (25 miles) from the Pakistani border.

- US Federal drug agents uncovered 50,000 pounds of marijuana hidden in a 'nondescript' house in Queens, New York, in 2009 as part of a crackdown on a drug-smuggling operation in neighbouring Canada. The street value was $150 million. Ten people were arrested.

- In Afghanistan in 2007, coalition forces uncovered £200 million worth of hash buried deep in an underground complex of trenches and bunkers. The haul was reportedly meant to help finance the Taliban in their war against the West.

- At the port of Riyadh, in Saudia Arabia, in 2010, almost 12,000 pounds of hashish worth in the region of $35 million was seized. Seven East Asian men and an Arab male were arrested in connection with the bust. Saudi Arabia is governed by Sharia law – which prescribes the death penalty for convicted drug traffickers.

- Law enforcement authorities in Houston, Texas, seized more than 19,000 pounds of hash stored inside two yellow school buses in a remote area south west of the city in March 2007. US Immigration and Customs agents estimated that the hash haul had a street value of almost $50 million.

- The Mexico-based 'Victor Emillio Cazares-Gastellum' drug trafficking gang was busted with 27,229 pounds of marijuana by US authorities in 2007. That and other drugs found by agents were given a conservative street value of $45.2 million. More than 400 members of the cartel were arrested and authorities confiscated $6 million in property assets, 100 weapons and 94 vehicles.

- A US Coast Guard unit discovered 26,000 pounds of hash aboard a 63-foot yacht *Arrakis*, in November, 1984. It was the largest West Coast bust up to that time and worth in excess of $10 million on the open market.

THE DIRTY DOZEN BIGGEST EVER HASH BUSTS

- In October, 2009, members of the British Army's Black Watch regiment in Afghanistan seized six tons of hash – including a block the size of a football pitch – during a three-day aviation assault mission to clear insurgent equipment from the Lakari Bazaar in the Garmsir district of American-controlled southern Helmand Province. The hash was said to be worth 'hundreds of millions of dollars' on the open market.

- A raid by the US Drug Enforcement Agency and Afghan counter-narcotics agents in July, 2012, in Afghanistan's Kandahar Province uncovered a massive underground bunker that contained approximately 3,125 kilograms of pre-packaged hashish and another 2,500 kilograms of marijuana worth more than $200 million on the open market.

- Canadian police in late 2010 arrested eight people and seized more than 43 tons of hashish with an estimated street value of CAN $860 million after raids in four different countries.

- Three Israelis were arrested in the British port of Southampton in April, 2008, on suspicion of trying to smuggle over six tons of hash into the country. Police at the time called it the UK's largest ever hash haul. The hash had been purchased for hundreds of thousands of dollars and was expected to fetch more than $15 million on the open market.

- Mexican hash traffickers built their own version of an underground railroad in 2011 to transport cannabis across the California–Mexico border. After following a suspicious truck to a Tijuana warehouse, police found the entrance to the freshly-excavated 1,800-foot long tunnel complete with a light rail system that smoothly delivered hash through a crawlspace on the Californian side. All in all, authorities seized 30 tons of hash worth $20 million.

COCAINE CONFIDENTIAL
TRUE STORIES BEHIND THE WORLD'S MOST NOTORIOUS NARCOTIC

Wensley Clarkson

Cocaine is the world's most notorious narcotic. It underpins a vast, multi-billion pound underworld with a dark and deadly side. But who really are the shadowy people behind this chilling network? The coca farmers, the jungle sweat-shop workers, the smugglers, the suppliers, and, ultimately, the dealers who provide for the world's hundreds of millions of users. *Cocaine Confidential* examines the lives of all these characters to reveal their stories for the first time.

Along the way you'll meet hitmen, coke barons, mules, hardened traffickers, desperate former international footballers, pimps and corrupt cops as the truth is unravelled in a roller coaster ride through this secret world.

Quercus
www.quercusbooks.co.uk

THE CURSE OF BRINK'S-MAT

Twenty-Five Years of Murder and Mayhem

Wensley Clarkson

On 26 November 1983 six armed robbers escaped with £28 million worth of gold bullion from a Brink's-Mat warehouse at London's Heathrow Airport. The heist changed the face of British crime for ever. In the following years, many of those involved, innocent and guilty alike, have been sent to an early grave. Two decades on, the death toll is still rising.

Nobody is better placed than Wensley Clarkson to track the vicious, violent and unexpected waves that followed in its wake, or bring to life its cast of larger-than-life characters. From small-time crime in south-east London, to 'the heist of the century' and its bloody consequences, Wensley Clarkson's *The Curse of Brink's-Mat* is an epic tale of villainy, gold and revenge.

Quercus
www.quercusbooks.co.uk